1996

The Utopian Vision of D. H. Lawrence

EUGENE GOODHEART

The Utopian Vision
of
D. H. Lawrence

The University of Chicago Press

Chicago and London

Acknowledgments are made to *The Letters of D. H. Lawrence*, *Phoenix*, *The Rainbow*, *Psychoanalysis and the Unconscious*, and *Fantasia of the Unconscious* by D. H. Lawrence, Viking Press, Messrs. William Heinemann, Ltd., Laurence Pollinger, Ltd., and the estate of the late Mrs. Frieda Lawrence, and to *Duino Elegies* by Rainer Maria Rilke, W. W. Norton & Co., Inc.

The University of Chicago Press, Chicago 60637
The University of Chicago Press, Ltd., London

© *1963 by The University of Chicago*
All rights reserved. Published 1963
Second Impression 1971
Printed in the United States of America

International Standard Book Number: 0–226–30288–1
Library of Congress Catalog Card Number: 63–22817

To My Mother and Father
and Pat

Acknowledgments

I want to thank Professors Lionel Trilling and Jacques Barzun of Columbia University for the considerable help I received from them while doing this study. I am particularly grateful to Professor Trilling, who provided the right resistance to my ideas and formulations. His criticisms, even at the most difficult stage of the work, were exacting without being discouraging. Professor Barzun's comments on the general conception of the study as well as those in the margins of the pages were very useful. I wish also to express my gratitude to Professor William York Tindall of Columbia, who read the manuscript at a later stage. My friend Ilya Wachs deserves special thanks for his critical acuity, his enormous help in preparing the manuscript, and his talent for giving encouragement when needed. Alvin C. Kibel and Baruch Hochman rendered their services in the preparation of the manuscript. I am even more grateful to them for the discussions about Lawrence and related matters. My wife, Patricia Somer Goodheart, who was a constant and helpful presence while I worked, enhanced the pleasure of my labors by so thoroughly participating in them.

Contents

Introduction

This study is a complex elaboration of what appears to be a simple thesis: that Lawrence's imagination was oriented toward the future, that its characteristic impulse was to discover new forms of life immanent, though not actual, in the world, and that his principal discovery was the bodily or physical life that he believed man had once possessed in his pre-civilized past and must now fully recover if future *civilized* life is to be possible. In the effort to reveal the revolutionary implications of Lawrence's utopianism both in his art and in his thought, I go against the prevailing tendency, most significantly exemplified by F. R. Leavis, to confine Lawrence within English ethical and artistic traditions.

My attention to Lawrence's utopianism does not yield a simplified version of his work. On the contrary, throughout the study there is a full recognition of the ambiguities of his achievement. In one sense he is the last great representative of the moral tradition of the English novel; in another, he is *sui generis*—without significant precedent. He is antichrist and he is "almost a Christian"; he is a diabolist in the service of the dark gods and he is one of the great instances of the English Protestant imagination; he is both the obsessed, compulsive artist whose vision was distorted by an unfortunate relationship with his mother and a writer committed to ideas of health and vitality. His view of society is paradoxical: on the one hand, he fiercely rejects its claim, and on the other, he sees his personal tragedy in the thwarting of his "societal" instinct. I have tried in this study to understand these oppositions as the expression of a single, coherent revolutionary imagination.

Since my interest is in Lawrence's total achievement, I have not followed the usual habit of Lawrence's critics of dividing my work into separate discussions of individual books. In all the chapters I move freely among his essays and his fiction. The first chapter aims at defining Lawrence's utopianism by placing it in a tradition of "tablet-breakers" (Nietzsche's phrase) and then considering some of the peculiar consequences it has for his art. The effort in the following chapters is to show the effect of Lawrence's utopianism on his views of nature, myth, and religious experience. Lawrence's ideas are not viewed as separate from his art; on the contrary, my attention is to the ways in which art and idea function—or fail to function—integrally in Lawrence's work. The study of his utopianism leads inevitably to his vision of "the greater life of the body," which is the subject of the fourth chapter. Of particular relevance to this vision is Nietzsche's conception of the Dionysian and the Apollonian as it is developed in *The Birth of Tragedy*. "The power-urge" which preoccupied Lawrence during the "dark period" of his career is shown to be no sudden invention of Lawrence's but the full emergence of the Dionysian theme which is present in almost all his work. Consequently, *Aaron's Rod* and *Kangaroo*, the novels of the "dark period," which are either ignored or disparaged by critics, are given serious attention in the fifth chapter. The theme of power becomes the basis of a fresh interpretation of *The Man Who Died*, the masterpiece of the final period. The chapter concludes with a discussion of Lawrence's version of the Christ story. Lawrence's bond with Jesus, the bond of one tablet-breaker with another, and his hostility to Christianity, already anticipated in the chapter on the religious character of his imagination, are discussed in connection with writers who were in a comparable relation to the Christian tradition: Blake, Dostoevsky, and Nietzsche. The study concludes with an emphasis on the visionary character of Lawrence's work and an evaluation of its importance for civilization.

Throughout this study, I have attempted to place Lawrence's achievement in relation to the central concerns of his time and to the intellectual and cultural movements with which his work has affinity. Blake, Nietzsche, Rilke, and Freud are among the writers and thinkers who appear and reappear in the study. Too much of the criticism of Lawrence has myopically isolated his achievement from its full historical and cultural context. Even F. R. Leavis, who has insisted for the past three decades on Lawrence's place in a tradition, has, by focusing exclusively on the pre-eminently English character of his work, failed to see his connections with European writers. To be sure, Lawrence's influence has been registered decisively on the Anglo-American consciousness, and his Englishness shows itself even at those moments when he has affinities with Nietzsche, but the Englishness hardly exhausts the definition of his achievement. And it is part of the effort of this study to create a wider context in which that achievement may be understood.

1

The Tablet-breaker

In recent years Lawrence has been made to serve causes not of his own choosing, notably the moral tradition of the English novel. The impetus for the remaking of Lawrence was initially provided by T. S. Eliot's attack on Lawrence in *After Strange Gods*, in which Eliot found the son of a Midlands coal-miner heretical and sinister, the inevitable result of a deficiency in the kind of tradition that a good education gives.[1] F. R. Leavis, coming to Lawrence's defense, argued insistently (sometimes impressively, often extravagantly) for Lawrence's place in "the great tradition" of the English novel.[2] Lawrence has been seen in relation to other worthy traditions. For instance, in one view, he is the last great writer who embodies the attack on machinery which began in England with Wordsworth and became so pervasive a theme in Victorian literature that Pater, surveying the whole of poetry, could define "all great poetry" as "a continual protest" against "the predominance of machinery.[3] There are real provocations for seeing Lawrence as traditional and moral.

---

[1] See T. S. Eliot, *After Strange Gods: A Primer of Modern Heresy* (London: Faber & Faber, Ltd., 1934), p. 58.

[2] See F. R. Leavis, *D. H. Lawrence: Novelist* (New York: Alfred A. Knopf, 1956).

[3] Walter Pater, *Appreciations* (London: Macmillan & Co., Ltd., 1924), p. 61.

If one reads *The Rainbow* for its depiction of the traditional ways of English country life, one is impressed with Lawrence's resemblance to the George Eliot of *Adam Bede*. The essay "Democracy" read without reference to his other works yields a social and morally earnest Lawrence not unlike the Carlyle of "Signs of the Times."

The unfortunate effect of underlining Lawrence's debts to tradition is that it tends to deprive him of the special claim that he makes upon us. His achievement has analogues in the history of literature—the achievements of Rousseau, Blake, Dostoevsky, Nietzsche, Rilke—but these analogues do not constitute a tradition in the meaning that usually attaches to the word. Continuity with the past, the handing-down of inherited cultural attitudes—tradition in this sense does not figure in Lawrence. He is rather, in the phrase of Nietzsche, one of "the tablet-breakers"[4] who appear at significant crises in culture and whose characteristic impulse is to divert the current of tradition into new and hitherto unknown channels.

Lawrence and the other tablet-breakers were men possessed with a prophetic vision; for them the past was interesting only for those moments that prefigured the future. There is no nostalgia for the past, no reverence for tradition in Lawrence's meditations on the painted tombs of Tarquinia, "the turgid muscularity" of the Etruscan figures or the Hopi snake dances.[5] Always in Lawrence there is the ulterior view of the future.

> We've got to rip the old veil of a vision across, and find what the heart really believes in, after all: and what the heart really wants, for the next future. And we've got to put it

---

[4] See Friedrich Nietzsche, *Thus Spake Zarathustra*, trans. Thomas Common, in *The Philosophy of Nietzsche* (New York: Modern Library, 1950), pp. 218–41.

[5] See D. H. Lawrence, *Mornings in Mexico* and *Etruscan Places*, Introduction by Richard Aldington (London: William Heinemann, Ltd., 1956).

down in terms of belief and of knowledge. And then go forward again, to the fulfillment in life and art.[6]

"The *next* future" is at the heart of Lawrence's quarrel with the past. He conceives of history as cyclical, not progressive. Like Blake and Nietzsche, Lawrence tried to unburden himself of the past;[7] he thought himself to be at the beginning of a new epoch. Of course, the belief in a future radically discontinuous from the past is an illusion. As Bergson remarks of the cyclical or "pendulum" theory of history:

> The pendulum is endowed with memory, and is not the same when it swings back as on the outward swing, since it is then richer by all the intermediate experience. This is why the image of a spiral movement, which has sometimes been used, is perhaps more correct than that of the oscillations of a pendulum.[8]

Moreover, even a new beginning must come out of something in the human past. As Karl Jaspers has pointed out, "if the breach in the continuity of history were allowed to be established, man would destroy himself."[9] In Jaspers' description of "a sincere historicity" we have a glimpse of the tablet-breaker's creative relationship to the past.

> That which is acquired as a new possession is something which transforms the present. The insincere historicity of a culture which does no more than understand is a mere will

---

[6] D. H. Lawrence, *Psychoanalysis and the Unconscious* and *Fantasia of the Unconscious*, Introduction by Philip Rieff (New York: Viking Press, 1960), p. 57. The above passage is from *Fantasia of the Unconscious*. Henceforth reference to this book will indicate only the essay from which a passage is quoted.

[7] Blake mythicized history in order to overcome it and Nietzsche conceived the possibility of the evolution of man into a higher species.

[8] Henri Bergson, *The Two Sources of Morality and Religion*, trans. R. A. Andra and Cloudesley Brereton (New York: Doubleday Anchor Books, 1957), p. 292.

[9] Karl Jaspers, *Man in the Modern Age*, trans. Eden and Cedar Paul (New York: Doubleday Anchor Books, 1957), p. 132.

to repeat the past; but a sincere historicity is a readiness to discover the sources which feed all life and therefore the life of the present as well.[10]

"The sincere historicity" is then nothing more than the freedom to discover in the past the possibilities of re-creating the present.

It is characteristic for the tablet-breaker to assume at various times the roles of nihilist, mystic, diabolist, and obscurantist, for the language of traditional thought and feeling would only give the lie to his grasp of the future. His refusal to assume traditional moral attitudes is not a refusal to be moral. On the contrary, the tablet-breaker has discovered immorality in the old attitudes, and, by assuming on occasion the mask of the immoralist, he attempts to express a new morality.

Since the new morality is a dialectical outgrowth of the old, its richness and cogency depend upon the profundity with which the immoralist has grasped the reality of what he sets out to destroy. In Lawrence's work the traditional attitudes are subjected to the most thoroughgoing scrutiny, so that rejecting the old and creating the new are experienced as necessity. Where Lawrence fails, imagination and intelligence have turned away splenetically from the necessary task of scrutinizing the old world. The result is stridency and thinness.

The view that Lawrence "was rejecting, not the claims of society, but the claims of industrial society"[11] mistakenly places him in a tradition that includes Carlyle, Ruskin, Arnold, and Morris. What distinguishes Lawrence's attack on mechanical civilization from that of the Victorian essayists is

---

[10] *Ibid.*

[11] Raymond Williams, *Culture and Society* (New York: Columbia University Press, 1958), p. 205.

his thoroughgoing vision of the character of social organization. The industrial organization of society merely exposed
its generic mechanical character. When imagined against the
teeming life of nature, the life of society shrinks to almost
nothing. "Upon the vast, incomprehensible pattern of some
primal morality greater than ever the human mind can grasp,
is drawn the little, pathetic pattern of man's moral life and
struggle, pathetic, almost ridiculous."[12] None of the Victorian writers, with the possible exception of Hardy, whose work
Lawrence is describing above, ever imagined a life beyond
society. Their quarrel with society was a quarrel with its
evils. Like the heroes of George Eliot's novels, they wanted
only the chance to serve society, to make it better. For them
the best claims of self and society are identical. The opposition between Lydgate (a man who wishes to serve the best
interests of society) and Middlemarch (a community unwill-
ing to be served) is a *locus classicus* for the period.

Despite his vision of the generic inadequacy of society to
fulfil human desires and aspirations, Lawrence—except in his
bitterest moods—never made a nihilistic rejection of society.
On the contrary, by refusing to perform his duty in society,
he was in a sense its truest champion. What we have in
Lawrence is the coincidence of two impulses: the impulse
toward *self-responsibility* (the phrase that he assigns to the
quests of his heroes in *Aaron's Rod* and *Kangaroo*) and the impulse toward true human community. When society demands
total commitment, it is in the very act of destroying itself;
to refuse to make the commitment then is a way of saving
society from itself.

---

[12] D. H. Lawrence, "Study of Thomas Hardy," *Phoenix: The Posthumous Papers of D. H. Lawrence*, ed. with an Introduction by E. D. McDonald (New
York: Viking Press, 1936), p. 419.

The Christian love, the brotherly love, this is always sacred. I love my neighbor as myself. What then? I am enlarged, I surpass myself. I become whole in mankind [read *society*]. In the whole of perfect humanity I am whole. I am the microcosm, the epitome of the great microcosm. . . .

Then I shall hate the self that I am, powerfully and profoundly shall I hate this microcosm that I have become, this epitome of mankind. I shall hate myself with madness the more I persist in adhering to my achieved self of brotherly love.

There must be brotherly love, a wholeness of humanity. But there must also be pure, separate individuality, separate and proud as a lion or a hawk.[13]

This is one of the "secrets" of Lawrence's performance as a *social critic*—a phrase inadequate to the radical nature of his criticism. He is in constant sensitive reaction against the thousand subtle ways in which society seeks to establish its precedence in human life, because society itself will be corroded by the self-hatred of its members, if the single, isolate life of man will not be given equal sway.

The basis of Lawrence's "social criticism" is a passionate quarrel—it is also Blake's quarrel in *The Prophetic Books*—with the dualism presupposed by life in society. The opposition between impulse and obligation, personal right and law—which is the preoccupation of so much of Western literature and thought—is dissolved in Lawrence's conception of spontaneous being. For Lawrence society is not a system of obligations, a necessary social contract into which one enters unwillingly; it is the fulfilment of the human *impulse* toward community with others. In a letter Lawrence characterized his personal tragedy as the consequence of the thwarting of his "societal" instinct, which he felt to be deeper than the

---

[13] "Love," *ibid.*, pp. 155–56.

sexual instinct.[14] The concern with community and citizen-
ship in "Education of the People" reflects a fear about
what happens to the spontaneous life of a person in a period
of social disintegration, when connections with others become impossible.[15]

The appeal to spontaneity to decide the issues of life is
the only recourse the tablet-breaker has to overcome the
dualisms of life and culture, the self and the world. He is deaf
to the claims of the world and culture, because to grant them
a hearing is to tolerate the dualism. Every impulse of the
tablet-breaker is devoted to restoring culture to life, the
world to the self. The great task for the utopian reconstruction of society that Lawrence undertakes is to discover and
present in his work the content of "the profound spontaneous
soul of men."[16]

Lawrence conceives all human relationships, personal,
familial, and social, in "the spontaneous mode."

> The actual evolution of the individual psyche is a result of
> the interaction between the individual and the outer universe.
> Which means that just as a child in the womb grows as a re-
> sult of the parental blood-stream which nourishes the vital
> quick of the foetus, so does every man and woman grow and
> develop as a result of the polarized flux between the spon-
> taneous self and some other self or selves.[17]

By spontaneity Lawrence does not mean giving free rein to
the impulses. He means rather a dialectic within the spontaneous mode itself between impulse and resistance.

> Because there is no primary resistance in us, nothing . . .
> resists the helpless but fatal flux of ideas which streams us

---

[14] D. H. Lawrence, *The Letters of D. H. Lawrence*, ed. with an Introduction
by Aldous Huxley (London: William Heinemann, Ltd., 1956), p. 685.

[15] See *Phoenix*, pp. 587–669.

[16] *Ibid.*, p. 611.   [17] *Psychoanalysis and the Unconscious*, p. 46.

away. The resistant spontaneous centers have broken down
in us.[18]

Without resistance (a spontaneous action of the will), individual being is impossible.

In the essay on education and the two books on psychoanalysis, Lawrence shows in detail how the infant is social-
ized through a *spontaneous* interaction with his parents. The
child for Lawrence is "soft and vulnerable," and it "is our
responsibility to see that this unformed thing shall come to
its own final form and fullness, both physical and mental."[19]
Lawrence's principal lesson is to leave the child alone, i.e.,
teach it to be alone.

> Break the horrible circle of . . . lust. . . . Seize babies away
> from their mothers, with hard, fierce, terrible hands. Send the
> volts of fierce anger and severing force violently into the
> child. . . . Drive them back from their yearning, loving para-
> sitism.[20]

Indeed, so keen is Lawrence's mistrust of the tendency of
modern parents to encourage the "yearning, loving parasitism
of their children," and consequently unman them, that he
fails to recognize fully the equally pernicious tendency of
parents to inhibit affection and tenderness. Anger, even violent anger directed toward the child, defines him, whereas
affection tends to dissolve the bonds of personality. If the
child is to grow up to be a man, the parent must be spontaneous. Lawrence distrusts every "idealistic" inhibition of the
parent's impulses toward the child.

> We must accept the bond of parenthood primarily as a
> vital, mindless conjunction, non-ideal, passional. A parent
> *owes* the child all the natural passional reactions provoked. If
> a child provokes anger, then to deny this anger, the open pas-

---

[18] "Education of the People," *Phoenix*, p. 629.
[19] *Ibid.*   [20] *Ibid.*, pp. 639–40.

sional anger, is as bad as to deny it food or love. It causes an atrophy in the child, at the volitional centres, and a perversion of the true life-flow.[21]

The goal of education is "independence, independence, self-independence."[22] In "Education of the People" Lawrence proposes a definite educational program that will prepare the child for life in society.

> All education should be state education. All children should start together in the elementary schools. From the age of seven to the age of twelve boys and girls of every class should be educated together in the elementary schools. This will give us a common human basis, a common radical understanding. All children, boys and girls, should receive training in the respective male and female crafts. Every man should finally be expert in some craft, and should be trained a free soldier, no matter what his profession. Every woman also should have her chosen expert craft, so that each individual is master of some kind of work.[23]

Though the work that absorbs the consciousness is "quite a pleasant occupation for a human creature, a natural activity,"[24] it plays a subordinate role in Lawrence's utopia. Despite the necessity and pleasure of work, "it is still a state which every man hopes release from."[25] Creative activity is of a different order. The spontaneous creative act differs radically from work, which is finally mere mechanical repetition. In his carving, Will Brangwen (in *The Rainbow*) is performing a creative act: he is "being himself . . . producing himself."[26]

It is significant that Lawrence does not conceive of an opposition between work and play, as do Freud and other writ-

---

[21] *Ibid.*, pp. 646–47.
[22] *Ibid.*, p. 648.
[23] *Ibid.*, p. 598.

[24] *Ibid.*, p. 648.
[25] *Ibid.*, p. 424.
[26] *Ibid.*, p. 429.

ers who derive their premises from Freud.[27] As in the conflict between impulse and obligation, the opposition between work and play is an intolerable condition of life in a "repressive" society, another version of the dualism that Lawrence, the tablet-breaker, seeks to overcome. It is as if he understood that play was the ideal imagined under the stress of repressive work and that in a society in which one was free to be oneself, indeed to become a self, the division between work and play would be meaningless. Lawrence in his own life was free of that yearning for leisure and play that is characteristically modern. Richard Aldington describes Lawrence's attitude toward games in the following manner:

> Again he won my approval by his total indifference to sports of all sorts. Since he lived intensely, since his mind was perpetually active and his senses acutely employed, he had no need to kill time by killing animals or birds or by propelling balls in competitive feats or by glowering over indoor games. Superior even to the great Gibbon, he never felt it necessary to relax over a game of cards. Is life so long, is the mind so dull, is there so little to see and do and feel and know, that we must waste the unique (if diabolical) gift of consciousness in silly games? If anyone presented Lawrence with a golf-ball or a cricket-bat he would have cracked him over the head with it.[28]

Activity in "the daylight world"[29]—the utopian world of men engaged in heroic and creative action, as Lawrence conceives it in *Fantasia of the Unconscious*—is purposive and selfless, a spontaneous giving-up of oneself to the life of the community. But the surrender of the self, in Lawrence's view, is

---

[27] See, for example, Herbert Marcuse, *Eros and Civilization: A Philosophical Inquiry into Freud* (Boston: Beacon Press, 1955).

[28] Edward Nehls (ed.), *D. H. Lawrence: A Composite Biography* (3 vols.; Madison: University of Wisconsin Press, 1956–59), III, 458–59.

[29] This phrase is used in *Fantasia of the Unconscious* and elsewhere.

not an obligation or a duty: it is the fulfilment "of the great urge that is upon [a man]."

> We have got to get back to the great purpose of manhood, a passionate unison in actively making a world. . . . in the commingling of a passionate purpose each individual sacredly abandons his individuality. . . . He knows what he does. He makes the surrender honourably, in agreement with his own soul's deepest desire. But he surrenders, and remains responsible for the purity of his surrender.[30]

Lawrence's very language is an attempt to alter the way in which we characteristically conceive the individual's life in society. The great urge upon the self to activity is no mechanical, compulsive action of the will which yields neither pleasure nor fulfilment; it is directed toward the fulfilment of man's highest nature.

II

Lawrence's effort to reconceive human life in "the spontaneous mode" has remarkable artistic and philosophical consequences. If, as Lawrence himself believed, "the artistic effort is the effort of utterance, the supreme effort of expressing knowledge, that which has been once, that which was enacted, where the two wills met and left their result, complete for the moment,"[31] then Lawrence's imaginative venturing-forth into life yet to be enacted, the knowledge of which is still to come, has given art new tasks.[32] Indeed, Lawrence's whole

---

[30] *Fantasia of the Unconscious*, p. 144.

[31] "Study of Thomas Hardy," *Phoenix*, p. 447.

[32] In Stephen Dedalus' diary in *A Portrait of the Artist as a Young Man* there is an entry about one of Yeats's poems which, for all the opposition between Joyce and Lawrence, strikingly illuminates Lawrence's imaginative intention. "Michael Robartes remembers forgotten beauty and, when his arms wrap her round, he presses in his arms the loveliness which has long faded from the world. Not this. Not at all. I desire to press in my arms the loveliness which has not yet come into the world." James Joyce, *The Portable Joyce*, ed. with an Introduction by Harry Levin (New York: Viking Press, 1957), p. 523.

imaginative career is a repudiation of art which is content to imitate already enacted life. The difference between, say, Aldous Huxley and Lawrence is the difference between satire, which despite its critical vision is nevertheless committed to the reality it satirizes, and imaginative adventure in which the imagination seeks to transcend the old life. Whitehead is most illuminating here:

> Satire is the last flicker of originality in a passing epoch as it faces the onroad of staleness and boredom. Freshness has gone: bitterness remains. The prolongation of outworn forms of life means a slow decadence in which there is repetition without any fruit in the reaping of value.[33]

The agent of significant change from the moribund forms of civilization to new and vital forms is man's spirit of adventure, which "reaches beyond the safe limits of learned rules of taste."[34] Lawrence chose the way of adventure; the impulse of his imagination was always to be at "the extreme tip of life,"[35] where, in the words of Whitehead, adventure "produces the dislocations and confusions marking the advent of new ideals for civilized effort."[36]

Thus when Lawrence speaks of the banality of Thomas Mann, he is identifying a kind of art which is anathema to his belief in the future and his desire for change. Lawrence, however, fails to do Mann full justice—and hence fails to do justice to the important defining difference between Mann and himself—when he characterizes him as "the last sick sufferer from the complaint of Flaubert," who "regarded life as a disordered corruption, against which he can fight with only one weapon, his fine aesthetic sense, his feeling for beauty, for

---

[33] Alfred North Whitehead, *Adventures of Ideas* (New York: Macmillan Co., 1937), p. 360.
[34] *Ibid.*, pp. 359–60.
[35] "Study of Thomas Hardy," *Phoenix*, p. 409.
[36] Whitehead, *Adventures of Ideas*, p. 360.

perfection . . . however corrupt the stuff of life may be."[37] It is the intention of "Death in Venice," the work which Lawrence is here reviewing, to expose the corrupt and perverse roots of the aesthete, who asserts his "fine aesthetic sense" and "feeling for beauty" against "the disordered corruption" of life. Indeed, "Death in Venice" gives us the most devastating vision of the perverse sources of aesthetic art. Mann, ostensibly in the aesthetic camp, is its most cunning enemy, for he has exposed aestheticism simply by unfolding its logic in a masterly way. Devoted to the creation of beautiful forms as the way to self-mastery, Gustave Aschenbach is betrayed by his susceptibility to sensuous beauty into lusts which undermine his self-mastery and finally cause his death. Lawrence attempted to render the aesthetic artist in his characterizations of Loerke in *Women in Love* and 'Rico in *St. Mawr*, but both attempts are mere sketches next to Mann's masterpiece. Whereas, however, the character of Aschenbach represents for Mann the range of possibilities for the artist in the modern world, Loerke and 'Rico belong, so to speak, to the debris of a dying world beyond which Lawrence's imaginative adventure is taking place. Lawrence, in other words, refuses to accept the limits of human experience as conceived by Mann.

The tragic dilemma in "Death in Venice" is that there is finally no choice between morality and passion. One leads to the other and both lead to death. Aschenbach's moral life is typical of those who "labor at the edge of exhaustion"[38]— lacking access to energy without which there is no genuine moral life. His exhaustion makes him prey to the passions that explode the necessary order of his existence. Mann evi-

---

[37] D. H. Lawrence, "German Books: Thomas Mann," *Phoenix*, p. 312.

[38] Thomas Mann, "Death in Venice," *Stories of Three Decades*, trans. H. T. Lowe Porter (New York: Alfred A. Knopf, 1948), p. 334.

dently means to make a statement about the eternal and mutually destructive opposition between morality and the passions. The tone of the narrative voice, detached and neutral with just the faintest suggestion of pathos, is the tone appropriate to a sense of tragic dilemma. If we regard "Death in Venice" as a work written not under the aspect of eternity but in time, then the moral of the tale is that death is the theme of a civilization which has become excessive in its moral demands.[39]

Mann's vision of the tragic opposition between morality and passion in which both are seen as destructive and disintegrative is a striking anticipation of Freud's tragic view in *Civilization and Its Discontents*,[40] and both books are, as it were, the negative evidence for Lawrence's utopian claims. According to Freud, the effort to control or sublimate the passions only stimulates their secret and insidious workings. Whatever harmony they appear to achieve from time to time, the instincts and the moral exigencies of civilization are ultimately irreconcilable. The identification in "Death in Venice" of passion with crime and disease depends on an opposition between morality and the passions. Mann remarks "the dark satisfaction" that Aschenbach derived from the knowledge that the plague had spread to Venice: "Passion is like crime; it does not thrive on the established order and the common round; it welcomes every blow dealt the bourgeois structure, every weakening of the social fabric, because therein it feels a sure hope of its own advantage."[41]

---

[39] Nietzsche's definition of morality can well stand as a motto for "Death in Venice": "Morality is the idiosyncrasy of the decadents actuated by a desire *to avenge themselves successfully* upon life." *Ecce Homo*, trans. Clifton P. Fadiman, in *The Philosophy of Nietzsche*, p. 931.

[40] Sigmund Freud, *Civilization and Its Discontents*, trans. Joan Riviere (New York: Jonathan Cape and Harrison Smith, 1930).

[41] Mann, "Death in Venice," p. 419.

Lawrence resolves the dilemma by conceiving the moral life as a direct expression of the passions. He imagines a world in which passion is not an explosive response to a repressive moral life but is permitted to issue freely from the solar plexus and find from moment to moment its appropriate forms. The free movement of energy is an essential condition for the creation of appropriate forms. Lawrence's utopianism presupposes a faith in the capacity of energy to get beyond "dislocations and confusions" when it surpasses its old habits. When Lawrence frees his characters from social determinations, he frees them not for the sake of freedom, but in order to permit their explorations of the possibilities of genuine moral life.[42] The violent soul agonies of, say, Birkin, in *Women in Love*, are those of a newly won freedom which has not yet found its appropriate form and which therefore is still without full moral power, and the moment of full moral power in the characters is, interestingly enough, expressed not through violence but through stillness—as in the scene in *Women in Love* in which Gerald and Gudrun are canoeing.

> "You like this, do you?" she said, in a gentle solicitous voice.
> He laughed shortly.
> "There is a space between us," he said, in the same low unconscious voice, as if something were speaking out of him. And she was as if magically aware of their being balanced in separation, in the boat. She swooned with acute comprehension and pleasure.

---

[42] Dostoevsky's Christianity has its origins in the passions. According to Berdyaev's interpretation of Dostoevsky's theology—an interpretation which I endorse—the good, for Dostoevsky, can never be a matter of compulsion or coercion. It must have its origins in freedom, and for this reason Dostoevsky is willing to take all the risks of freedom—the risks, for instance, of the perversities of the underground man. See Nicholas Berdyaev, *Dostoevsky* (New York: Meridian Books, 1959).

"But I'm very near," she said caressingly, gaily.
"Yet distant, distant," he said.[43]

Gerald and Gudrun have for the moment achieved the male-female polarity, in which in their real connection with each other they still maintain their individual identities. The stillness of the moment is their achievement of moral being, an achievement possible only in a state of freedom. "The best thing I have known," Lawrence remarks in a confidential mood in *Fantasia of the Unconscious*, "is the stillness of accomplished marriage, when one possesses one's own soul in silence, side by side with the amiable spouse, and has left off craving and raving and being only half of one's self."[44]

Nietzsche's conception of the relationship between reason and the passions is similar to Lawrence's view of moral being as the *formal* realization of the passions. In *The Will to Power* Nietzsche speaks of "the misunderstanding of passion and reason [read *morality*], as if the latter existed as an entity by itself, and not rather as a state of the relations between different passions and desires; as if every passion did not contain in itself its own quantum of reason."[45] When reason (or morality) and the passions are in opposition to each other, there is finally neither genuine morality nor genuine passion. Both become the objects of suspicion. Thus Lawrence begins his essay on psychoanalysis with a chapter entitled "Psychoanalysis vs. Morality," in which he means to demonstrate that the psychoanalytic mistrust of both repression and the unconscious leads to the destruction of the moral sense, and

---

[43] D. H. Lawrence, *Women in Love*, Introduction by Richard Aldington (London: William Heinemann, Ltd., 1957), pp. 168–69.

[44] *Fantasia of the Unconscious*, p. 169.

[45] Quoted in Walter Kaufmann, *Nietzsche: Philosopher, Psychologist, Anti-Christ* (New York: Meridian Books, Inc., 1959), p. 203.

"that we can never recover our moral footing until we can in some way determine the true nature of the unconscious."[46] If, as Nietzsche remarks, "morality (the morality that opposes itself to the instincts), the Circe of mankind, has falsified everything psychological, from beginning to end,"[47] then there must be a probing of the unconscious without moral preconceptions. Lawrence is an immoralist (in the Nietzschean sense) in rejecting what Nietzsche calls "morality-in-itself."[48] For Nietzsche and Lawrence the idea of the good when it is anterior to a knowledge of psychology, of "what the heart really wants," is pseudo or decadent morality.

The consequence of this for literature is made clear again by Nietzsche when he describes "the condition of the existence of good [as] falsehood," as "the unwillingness to see how reality is actually constituted."[49] Lawrence's utopianism, from this point of view, is a species of realism. When Lawrence turns from the old world, the social world, to discover "new emotions . . . a whole new line of feeling,"[50] he is, as it were, turning from unreality to reality. And when he says of people that they are dead, he means more than the ordinary metaphorical meaning that generally attaches to such a statement. Lawrence has pierced the phantasmal life of people and events and has seen the death, the nullity, in them. The problem for Lawrence is to transcend the conventions by which the novel has traditionally apprehended reality in order to see "how reality is actually constituted."

In a letter written to his publisher and friend, Edward Garnett, Lawrence describes *The Rainbow* as the novel in

---

[46] *Psychoanalysis and the Unconscious*, p. 10.
[47] Nietzsche, *Ecce Homo*, in *The Philosophy of Nietzsche*, p. 861.
[48] *Ibid.*, p. 926.
[49] *Ibid.*
[50] "Surgery for the Novel—or a Bomb," *Phoenix*, p. 520.

which he discovered a new way to present his vision of reality.

I don't think the psychology is wrong, it is only that I have a different attitude to my characters, and that necessitates a different attitude in you, which you are not prepared to give. As for its being my cleverness which would pull the thing through—that sounds odd to me, for I don't think I am so very clever, in that way. I think the book is a bit futuristic—quite unconsciously so. But when I read Marinetti—"The profound intuitions of life added one to the other, word by word, according to their illogical conception, will give us the general psychology of an intuitive physiology of matter"—I can see something of what I am after. I translate him clumsily, and his Italian is often obfuscated—and I don't care about physiology of matter—but somehow—that which is physic—non-human, in humanity, is more interesting to me than the old fashioned element—which causes one to conceive a character in a certain moral scheme and make him consistent. The certain moral scheme is what I object to. In Turgenev, and in Tolstoi, and in Dostoevsky, the moral scheme into which all the characters fit—and it is nearly the same scheme —is, whatever the extraordinariness of the characters themselves, dull, old, dead. When Marinetti writes: "It is the solidity of a blade of steel that is interesting by itself, that is, the uncomprehending and inhuman alliance of its molecules in resistance to, let us say, a bullet. The heat of a piece of wood or iron is in fact more passionate for us, than the laughter or tears of a woman"—then I know what he means. He is stupid, as an artist, contrasting the heat of the iron and the laugh of the woman. Because what is interesting in the laugh of the woman is the same as the binding of the molecules of steel or their action in heat: it is the inhuman will, call it physiology, or like Marinetti—physiology of matter, that fascinates me. I don't so much care about what the woman feels—in the ordinary usage of the word. That presumes an ego to feel with. I only care about what the woman is—what she is—inhumanly, physiologically, materially—according to the use of the word. . . . You mustn't look in my novel for the old stable *ego* of the character. There is another *ego*, according to whose action the individual is unrecognizable, and passes through, as it were, allotropic states which it needs a deeper sense than any we've been used to exercise, to discover are states of the same single radically unchanged element. (Like as diamond and coal are the same pure single element of carbon. The ordinary novel would trace the history of the diamond—but I say, "Diamond, what! This is carbon." And my diamond might be coal or soot, and my theme is carbon.) . . .[51]

The characters of "the traditional novel" have two main alternatives to the tyranny of "the moral scheme." They can stand apart and refuse through the exercise of irony or introspection the scheme of which they are, nevertheless, ineluctably a part: this is the exercise of personality. Or, they can, like the heroine of Jane Austen's *Mansfield Park*, avoid the burden of personality and incarnate in their own beings the moral scheme. There is a third alternative: the way of Anna Karenina, Emma Bovary, and Jude Fawley, the way of open defiance and—because the moral scheme always retains its primacy—of doom.

Lawrence presents still another alternative. He means to reconceive character in such a way that the character no longer depends for his life on the moral scheme. In order to do this, he must reject the idea of personality, which divides the self between its social being and its private essence, thereby depriving the self of the *integrity* necessary to its freedom. The doctrine that the heroine of Jane Austen's *Sense and Sensibility* pronounces embodies that aspect of the novel against which Lawrence is reacting when he speaks of the traditional psychology of the novel.

---

[51] *The Letters of D. H. Lawrence*, pp. 197–98.

"But I thought it was right, Elinor," said Marianne, "to be guided wholly by the opinion of other people. I thought our judgments were given us merely to be subservient to those of our neighbors. This has always been your doctrine, I am sure."

"No, Marianne, never. My doctrine has never aimed at the subjection of the understanding. All I have ever attempted to influence has been the behaviour. You must not confound my meaning. I am guilty, I confess, of having often wished you to treat our acquaintance in general with greater attention; but when have I advised you to adopt their sentiments or conform to their judgment in serious matters?"[52]

Elinor's emphasis falls on the social ethic and diverts our attention from the implicit opposition between the private and the social (in Elinor's language, "the understanding" and "the behaviour"). The novel classically has been concerned with this opposition. Stendhal, for instance, whose point of view is at the opposite pole from Jane Austen's, conceives the same opposition in *The Red and the Black*—though in valuing Julien Sorel's private imagination, he is affirming the other term of the opposition. Both *Sense and Sensibility* and *The Red and the Black* reflect in their different ways a view of the inherent division of the self from the world, and both novels probe the possibility of overcoming the division. Elinor, the heroine of *Sense and Sensibility*, counsels courtesy and consideration in one's behavior in order to make social life possible, while recognizing "the understanding" as the domain of privacy. Sorel, in Stendhal's novel, puts on the mask of respectability in order both to succeed in society and to protect his dangerous imagination of glory from assault by society. In both novels, despite the different points

---

[52] Jane Austen, *Sense and Sensibility*, in *The Novels of Jane Austen* (New York: Modern Library, n.d.), p. 56.

of view of the novelists, there is no happy resolution of the tension that exists between the private and the social. Marianne almost dies and then makes a sorry peace with her world, and Sorel chooses death as the only way to end the divisions that mark his life.

The increasing psychological orientation of the novel in its historical development into the present century represents, from this point of view, an effort to resolve the opposition between the private and the social by creating a relatively insulated world of privacy. When the social world breaks into the novels of Proust or Joyce, it is assimilated to their peculiar psychological modes. Lawrence repudiates "the psychological novel" because he regards it not as an imaginative freeing of the self from its social bonds, but as a symptom of the impotence and disintegration of the modern self:

> it is self-consciousness, picked into such fine bits that the bits are most of them invisible, and you have to go by the smell. Through thousands and thousands of pages Mr. Joyce and Mrs. Richardson tear themselves to pieces, strip their smallest emotions to the finest threads, till you feel you are sewed inside a wool mattress that is being slowly shaken up, and you are turning to wool along with the rest of the woolliness.[53]

For Lawrence the modern psychological novel is the culminating expression of the estrangement of the self from the world that the novel has documented from the very beginning of its career.

In order "to explode this scheme of things," in order "to present us with really new feelings . . . new emotions which will get us out of the emotional rut,"[54] Lawrence defines his characters not by their complex relations to "the moral

---

[53] "Surgery for the Novel—or a Bomb," *Phoenix*, p. 518.

[54] *Ibid.*, p. 520.

scheme," but by the subtly intuited rhythms of the "physiology" of their psyche. The peculiar felicity of Lawrence's appropriation of the futurist Marinetti's phrase "the general psychology of an intuitive physiology of matter" is that its boldness suggests the kind of leap that Lawrence is making in conceiving character. "The inhuman, the physiological, the material"—Lawrence's paradoxical language proposes the extraordinary imaginative effort that must be made in order to recover energies which will restore vitality and plasticity to human life. Lawrence preserves his connection with the tradition of the novel—indeed he implies in effect that he alone of his contemporaries is discharging the sacred obligations of the novelist by insisting that the novel, like every other living thing in the world, cannot be limited to a single intention or definition. In Lawrence's view the novel, unlike other cultural expressions, is alive and changeful.

> Philosophy, religion, science, they are all of them busy nailing things down, to get a stable equilibrium. Religion, with its nailed-down One God, who says *Thou shalt, Thou shan't,* and hammers home every time; philosophy with its fixed ideas; science with its "laws": they, all of them, all the time, want to nail us down to some tree or other.
>
> But the novel, no. The novel is the highest example of subtle inter-relatedness that man has discovered. Everything is true in its own time, place, circumstance. . . . If you try to nail anything down, in the novel, either it kills the novel, or the novel gets up and walks away with the nail.[55]

III

The vital states of feeling and being in *The Rainbow* require, of course, a new vocabulary in which the "inhuman" or "material" element is prominent. A typical instance is Will's courtship of Anna:

---

[55] "Morality and the Novel," *Phoenix*, p. 528.

He spoke to his uncle and aunt that night. "Uncle," he said, "Anna and me think of getting married."

"Oh, ay!" said Brangwen.

"But how, you have no money?" said the mother.

The youth went pale. He hated these words. But he was like a gleaming, bright pebble, something bright and inalterable. He did not think. He sat there in his hard brightness and did not speak.[56]

And shortly afterward:

Will Brangwen went home strange and untouched. He felt he could not alter from what he was fixed upon, his will was set. To alter it he must be destroyed. He had no money. But he would get some from somewhere, it did not matter. He lay awake for many hours, hard and clear and unthinking, his soul crystallizing more inalterably. Then he went fast asleep.

It was as if his soul had turned into hard crystal. He might tremble and quiver and suffer, it did not alter.[57]

"Hard brightness," "soul crystallizing," "hard crystal": all this comes perilously close to jargon, but the phrases are essential to Lawrence's new intention. The conflicts and tensions in the first two generations of the Brangwens occur spontaneously. Scruples, duties, and restraints as they have played a part in the English and European novel are absent from *The Rainbow*. The action of the novel occurs in "the spontaneous mode." Vibrations, polarity, dynamic flow, and crystallization constitute the new vocabulary of relationship. The old vocabulary of manners and morals is superseded.

Society is conceived mythically as "the far-off world of cities and governments and the active scope of man, the magic land, where secrets were made known and desires

---

[56] D. H. Lawrence, *The Rainbow*, Introduction by Richard Aldington (London: William Heinemann, Ltd., 1957), p. 121.

[57] *Ibid.*

fulfilled."[58] This is no society that Lawrence has ever known. It is imagined as an opportunity for self-fulfilment. The particular society of the Brangwens, the farm community of the Erewash valley, is, significantly, vague and shadowy in its external presentation.[59] The "realism" of the novel—the mining towns, the Christmas celebration—protects Lawrence's conception of community from ever becoming vacuous. The community of *The Rainbow* is essentially Lawrence's invention, and it is invented at a moment when the possibility of living community has virtually died, a fact to which Lawrence is a constant witness in the books that follow *The Rainbow*. The utopian character of the society of *The Rainbow* can be seen at once when we compare it with *Adam Bede*, a novel to which *The Rainbow* bears resemblance. When George Eliot describes realistically the detail of life on the Poyser farm, she is imagining the hard, resistant facts against which the characters must define themselves. The tragedy of Hetty and Arthur is not the result of a violation of natural law as George Eliot would have us believe; it is rather in their failure to do their duty by the facts of social life. George Eliot begins with society and imagines character within it. Lawrence, on the other hand, begins with the individual and imagines his fulfilment. Society is ideally one opportunity for self-fulfilment.

Lawrence's utopianism is in his open disrespect for the hard, irreducible facts of social life. For instance, though he values Hardy for his power of presenting "the leafy, sappy passion and sentiment of the woodlands,"[60] the explosive

---

[58] *Ibid.*, p. 3.

[59] Lawrence characterized the manner of *The Rainbow* as follows: "It is quite different in manner from my other stuff—far less visualized" (*The Letters of D. H. Lawrence*, p. 105).

[60] "Study of Thomas Hardy," *Phoenix*, p. 419.

moments in a character when passion bursts out wildly, he refuses to recognize the validity of Hardy's perception of the failure of those moments to establish themselves as the final reality. The tight convention, which is the community in its practical and moral form, has in Hardy's view a reality that cannot be overcome by a trip to Australia or Etruscan places.

The novel has never been utopian in this sense. It has in fact been the glorious achievement of the novel to render those hard, resistant facts in a man's life. The free action of a character is defined *against* these facts—it is in the rising above the facts to which his life in one way or other is inextricably bound. In *The Rainbow* these facts have lost their resistance. A character's freedom is his potency, and the life of the novel the potencies of all the characters. (Thus "the Brangwens came and went without fear of necessity, working hard because of the life that was in them, not for want of the money."[61])

In the final section of *The Rainbow*, in which Ursula is the central figure, the utopian vision gives way to the social world as we know it, "the potent unrealities."[62] We are out of the magic circle of the first two generations of Brangwens. The circle widens and draws into itself the industrial town, the military life, the daily mechanical routine of teaching. Despite the atmosphere of "nullity," the utopian feeling remains. Indeed, it is the incapacity of the novel to register anything of the society beyond its nullity, its sheer oppressive emptiness that reflects its utopianism. Here is a characteristic description of Tom Brangwen's mine:

> The place had the strange desolation of a ruin. Colliers hanging about in gangs and groups, or passing along the as-

---

[61] *The Rainbow*, p. 1.   [62] *Ibid.*, p. 308.

phalt pavements heavily to work, seemed not like living people, but like spectres. The rigidity of the blank streets, the homogeneous amorphous sterility of the whole suggested death rather than life. There was no meeting place, no centre, no artery, no organic formation. There it lay, like the new foundations of a red-brick confusion rapidly spreading, like a skin-disease. . . .

The whole place was just unreal, just unreal. Even now, when he had been there for two years, Tom Brangwen did not believe in the actuality of the place. It was like some gruesome dream, some ugly, dead, amorphous mood become concrete.[63]

And again, while Ursula and Skrebensky are walking along the banks of a river, they are aroused by the light of the town. Ursula "in her sensual arrogance" denies the town any reality.

"It does not exist really. It rests upon the unlimited darkness, like a gleam of colored oil on dark water, but what is it —nothing, just nothing."[64]

The resistant facts on which the lives of the characters of novels by Balzac, Flaubert, and Tolstoy founder are reduced to nothingness in *The Rainbow*, so that Ursula is able to see a glorious future beyond the emptiness and pain of her present life.

And the rainbow stood on the earth. She knew that the sordid people who crept hard-scaled and separate on the face of the world's corruption were living still, that the rainbow was arched in their blood and would quiver to life in their spirit, that they would cast off their horny cover of disintegration, that new clean bodies would issue to a new germination, to a new growth, rising to the light and the wind and the clean rain of heaven. She saw in the rainbow the earth's new architecture, the old brittle corruption of houses and factories

---

[63] *Ibid*., pp. 334–35. [64] *Ibid*., pp. 447–48.

swept away, the world built up in a living fabric of Truth, fitting to the overarching heaven.[65]

Ursula, in her vision of "the new clean bodies" that will emerge from "the old brittle corruption" of the actual world, has in the breathtaking ending of the novel simply disengaged the self from the forms it takes in the social setting. Out of his utopian faith, Lawrence has reversed the argument of literary naturalism which presents man as a social creature: society is—or should be—the creature of man. Wherever society appears in the novel as an external entity rather than as the fulfilment of man's need for community, it is rendered as *nullity*. In Lawrence's metaphysics, the difference between the self and society, between the passions and mental consciousness, is the difference between reality and appearance.

The sanction for Lawrence's refusal to confer reality on the social world and social being is an experience common to our century and anticipated in the nineteenth century by writers like Flaubert, Dostoevsky, and Nietzsche. Toward the end of "Notes from the Underground," Dostoevsky's paradoxicalist foreshadows what is to become a major theme in modern literature when he remarks that "we do not even know where we are to find real life."[66] The reality that has been lost and to which the underground man appeals is the reality that Lawrence hopes to recover for civilized man.

> We find it hard to be men, men of *real* flesh and blood, *our own* flesh and blood. We are ashamed of it. . . . We are still-born, and for a long time we have been begotten not by living fathers, and that's just what we seem to like more and more.

---

[65] *Ibid.*, p. 495.

[66] Fyodor Dostoevsky, "Notes from the Underground," in *The Best Short Stories of Dostoevsky*, trans. with an Introduction by David Magarshack (New York: Modern Library, n.d.), p. 240.

. . . Soon we shall invent some way of being somehow or other begotten by an idea. . . .[67]

In the nightmare world of the underground man, flesh and blood reality is a utopian dream or the hopeless imagination of a lost world. The anomaly of Lawrence's achievement is that this utopian dream is imagined as reality at the moment when literature is principally concerned with documenting the experience of alienation and unreality.

The experience of alienation has created a predicament for the modern artist. Uncertain of the nature of reality, he has been forced to adopt "creative strategies"[68] which either dramatize that uncertainty or become a means of grasping reality. Thus, as if to confirm the underground man's experience of the human world as unreal, Kafka in *Metamorphosis* imagines the transformation of a man into a bug as a real event (thereby fulfilling the underground man's wish to become an insect). So real is the event that it is not apprehended as symbolic. As with every other fact in the tale, there is no distance between image and meaning. *Metamorphosis* is a radical instance of the modern preoccupation with "creative strategy" as a means of achieving knowledge of reality, however despairing. *The Rainbow*, at the opposite pole of affirmation and celebration, is another radical instance.

Sometimes art is inadequate to the purpose of rendering the life within the writer or the life within the characters whom the writer is imagining, but the moment of inadequacy instructs the artist in humility. Art cannot do everything, and it can do nothing unless it is humbly in the service of life. Lawrence does not share the rationalism of Tolstoy, who

[67] *Ibid.*, p. 240.
[68] See Philip Rahv, Introduction to *The Short Novels of Tolstoy*, trans. Aylmer Maude (New York: Dial Press, 1956).

believed that the world was intelligible enough to be completely grasped by a classical art. Lawrence's imagination dwells on what Whitehead in his pages on the romantic poets calls "the brooding presences in nature."[69] The objects in Lawrence's world are not discrete or clear in their outlines as they are in Tolstoy's world. Moreover, Lawrence is forever impressed with the inadequacy of the word to the task of communicating a full sense of those presences. Language for Lawrence is as suggestive and as evocative as possible, and its intention is to communicate a restless sense that there is a much greater world beyond it that it has only partially illuminated.

If Lawrence is opposed to the classicist presumption of a writer like Tolstoy, he is also opposed to the presumption of aestheticism, which in its exaltation of style—its belief in the unbounded potency of form—achieves an art paradoxically like classical art in being too satisfied with itself. Lawrence despises the Flaubertian passion for *le mot juste*, the satisfaction derived from making "a perfect [statement] in a world of corruption."[70] He has keenly perceived the life-hating animus of the artist's preoccupation with the perfection of form. Lawrence is unique among modern writers in his capacity to transcend the modern experience of unreality and alienation by discovering through a new mode of awareness a reality—which is not simply the artistic imagination itself—to which he could devote his artistic expression.

To be sure, Lawrence is not entirely free of the modern

---

[69] Alfred North Whitehead, *Science and the Modern World*, in *Alfred North Whitehead: An Anthology*, ed. with an Introduction by F. S. C. Northrop and Mason W. Gross (New York: Macmillan Co., 1953), pp. 430–39.

[70] D. H. Lawrence, "German Books: Thomas Mann," *Phoenix*, p. 312.

malaise. His art often suffers from the strain of imagining a life which every fact of our present life denies. The language of art requires concreteness for its success, and the language of the novel in particular must contain the hard fact of the world, even if poetically transmuted. Dickens' novels, which are poetic transmutations of the actual world both in their nightmare perception of it and in their envisioning of a Christian utopia, have as their bedrock the hard fact of the world. However much Dickens' imagination dwells upon the neat and well-lit rooms in Bleak House or the loving kindness of his Beatrice women, we are never permitted to forget the actual fog of London or the sewers that feed the Thames. Lawrence does not feel the same obligation to the actual. The movement into space in which men and women have passionate encounters is often not *realized* in the language. The rituals of his language—e.g., his addiction to the imagery of dark and light—often render his meaning intellectually and emotionally inaccessible. Here is one of the worst instances:

> She knew there was no leaving him, the darkness held them both and contained them, it was not to be surpassed. Besides, she had a full mystic knowledge of his suave loins of darkness, dark-clad and suave, and in this knowledge there was some of the inevitability and the beauty of fate, fate which one asks for, which one accepts in full.
>
> He sat still like an Egyptian Pharaoh, driving the car. He felt as if he were seated in immemorial potency, like the great carven statues of real Egypt, as real and as fulfilled with subtle strength, as these are, with a vague inscrutable smile on their lips. He knew what it was to have the strange and magical current of force in his back and loins, and down his legs, force so perfect that it stayed him immobile, and left his face subtly, mindlessly smiling. He knew what it was to be awake and potent in that other basic mind, the deepest

physical control, magical, mystical, a force in darkness like electricity.[71]

Such writing gives the impression of having been willed, not imagined. Sometimes the moment rendered is in its very nature undramatizable, and we are required to make a leap beyond art itself. The search for deeper and freer states of being in both *The Rainbow* and *Women in Love* results in the abstractness of the language that tries to render it.

R. P. Blackmur's strictures against "the fallacy of expressive form" in Lawrence are justified in view of Lawrence's refusal to be guided in his creative work by anything but his passions.[72] But they fail to locate the source of the fallacy. It is true that Lawrence believed that the form was present in feeling, and he refused to make the kind of conscious accommodation to his feeling that would have made him a greater artist. His refusal, however, is not the consequence of an aesthetic bias. It comes from his utopian impulse to dissolve the recalcitrant facts of reality, to achieve, in other words, states of being which would not be fixed by the fact or object. The fact or object would be present only as an opportunity for the movement of the self to greater being. Will Brangwen's "mystical" experience during his visit to Lincoln Cathedral is a splendid instance of this.

> Here the stone leapt up from the plain of earth, leapt up in a manifold, clustered desire each time, up, away from the horizontal earth, through twilight and dusk and the whole range of desire, through the swerving, the declination, ah to the . . . meeting, the clasp, the close embrace, the neutrality, the perfect swooning consummation, the timeless ecstasy, consummated.

---

[71] *Women in Love*, p. 310.

[72] See R. P. Blackmur, *Form and Value in Modern Poetry* (New York: Doubleday Anchor Books, 1957), pp. 253–85.

And there was no time nor life nor death, but only this, this timeless consummation, where the thrust from earth met the thrust from earth and the arch was locked on the keystone of ecstasy. This was all, this was everything. Till he came to himself in the world below. Then he gathered himself together, in transit, every jet of him strained and leaped, leaped clear into the darkness above, the fecundity and the unique mystery, to the touch, the clasp, the consummation, the climax of eternity, the apex of the arch.[73]

This episode is one of the most dramatic and most decisive moments in the novel, and its peculiar success illustrates the novelist's necessary commitment to the fact. When Lawrence tries to represent an action in the language of "mystical, magical force in darkness, like electricity," he fails because he has not conceived an action. The presence of Lincoln Cathedral, on the other hand, in all its concreteness and specificity becomes the occasion for an action. The fact is the necessary counterpoise to the impulse that tends to shatter character beyond recognizable being. We are reminded of Lawrence's own conception of spontaneous being as involving a dialectic between impulse and resistance. Without resistance, individual being is impossible. Lawrence fails when he dissolves the resistances of the space in which his characters live, when, in other words, he deprives his characters of the opportunities that their world offers.

The conflict between the Laurentian hero and the world is too often resolved by abolishing the world. The concomitant result is the annihilation of individuality for a mystic identification with the divine energy in the universe. Lawrence defended his conception of character by giving a new definition of individuality in contradistinction to personality.

---

[73] *The Rainbow*, p. 199.

An individual is that which is not divided or not dividable.
A *being* we shall not attempt to define, because it is indefinable. . . .

The old meaning lingers in *person*, and is almost obvious in
personality. A person is a human being as *he appears to others;*
and personality is that which is transmitted from the person
to his audience: the transmissible effect of man.[74]

But no definition can argue away the impression that Lawrence's people make when they are in the undivided state.[75]
They are simply not *there*—Lawrence's argument for them
illicitly does the work that his art should be doing. Indeed, it
constitutes an ironic reversal of his claim that his ideas are
simply the outgrowth of his art, that any art born of an idea
inevitably becomes lifeless. We respond, if we do respond,
not to the quality of being that is depicted, but to the argument for that quality. It is for this reason that there is so
much expository intellectual writing in the novels. We must
be told in *Women in Love* that Ursula and Birkin are connected
in a male-female polarity, for the actual consummations of
their passion are too often presented in a riot of language in
which distinction, separation, and division have no part. In
his radical conception of character as indefinable, Lawrence
becomes a victim of the malaise of the modern novel which
he has so graphically depicted. In his effort to imagine the
primal energies out of which selves are created, he frequently
loses the imagination of the self as finite, vital substance.

The kind of fact that is illustrated by Lincoln Cathedral
permits Lawrence full freedom of imagination without bringing him under the tyranny of the amorphous, from which his
work elsewhere suffers. What Lawrence's characters need

---

[74] "Democracy," *Phoenix*, p. 710.

[75] As we shall see, Lawrence made an heroic effort to reconceive the nature
of individual being. Admirable and interesting as the effort is, his dramatic conception of character suffers for it.

is not freedom—they possess that in abundance—but resistance. The landscape, the physical atmosphere of a place often generates the resistance that enables Lawrence to conceive characters as individual beings: the heavy oppressions of the heat in Mexico, the sinister brilliances of the sun in Australia, the sheer pain of being European in the strange mixtures of industrial civilization and the primitive heritage of Indian and aboriginal life that Australia and America embodied— these are typical instances. The opening chapter of *The Plumed Serpent* is a wonderful example of Lawrence's capacity for imagining individual being. Kate in her fascination, hysteria, and amusement at the bullfight never loses her individuality. It is for her the first in a series of experiences that will transform her into a creature of the Mexican dark gods, that will reduce her to a darkness out of which she emerges only when at moments she refuses to yield her old resistant self.

Lawrence's belief in the need for resistances against which the self is *realized* is compatible with the genius of the novel. If he has brought character beyond the frontiers of social and psychological experience with which the novel has been traditionally concerned—"the sharp knowing in apartness"[76] of Jane Austen's world and its mutations in the subsequent history of the novel—he has nevertheless imagined new resistances, new limiting facts in the very biological beings of the characters. Lawrence's failures are in the *hubris* of his passion for new experience, his failure against his better knowledge to keep his characters bound within their own ultimate limitations.

---

[76] D. H. Lawrence, "Apropos of *Lady Chatterley's Lover*," in *Sex, Literature and Censorship*, ed. with an Introduction by Harry T. Moore (New York: Viking Press, 1959), p. 109.

Art and Prophecy
The Mythical Dimension

"Never trust the artist, trust the tale."[1] Lawrence's *caveat* has been heeded by his critics, especially by those out of sympathy with his "message." The activities of artist and prophet (or moralist), so the argument goes, are mutually exclusive, and an artist who pursues both at once compromises his art. The first loyalty of any artist should be to his art, and Lawrence fails as artist when the "message" commands the loyalty instead. According to this view, and it is based on an influential aesthetic theory, Lawrence's ideas are interesting only insofar as they become an organic part of the aesthetic organization of the work. The ideas in themselves are of no interest to the literary critic. Thus a very able critic dismisses the claim of Lawrence's ideas to our critical attention. After a discussion of Lawrence's "love ethic," Eliseo Vivas discounts in effect the value of the discussion:

> But the central question is not the admissibility of Lawrence's "love ethic"—a problem which mature individuals ought to decide for themselves, if they are interested in it.

---

[1] D. H. Lawrence, *Studies in Classic American Literature* (New York: Doubleday Anchor Books, 1953), p. 5.

The central question is that Lawrence employs the novel to teach us a "love ethic": And by doing so he abandons the task of the artist and undertakes that of the propagandist.[2]

This objection to Lawrence rests, it seems to me, on a subtle confusion between two ideas. It is one thing to demand concreteness of a novel, that it supply the necessary imaginative evidence for whatever assertion is made about character or situation. (And certainly Mr. Vivas is persuasive in his case against *Aaron's Rod* and *Kangaroo*.) But it is quite another thing to refuse the artist the right to act through his art, to desire change in the world—and this is precisely what the mistrust of Lawrence's "message" amounts to. Literature as an action or an attack on the reader's consciousness is not original with Lawrence. Swift's terrible satires are not intended to be self-contained aesthetic performances. Informed by ideas, they are intended to be powerful lessons about the nature of mankind. And the paradoxes of Blake's *Marriage of Heaven and Hell* and Dostoevsky's *Notes from the Underground* are deliberate provocations to the reader's imagination and will, aimed at producing nothing less than a radical revision of the reader's consciousness.

The prophetic or moral intention in Lawrence is inextricably bound up with his art. One assumes an attitude of neutrality toward Lawrence's ideas, or, worse, one abstracts them from his art, at the cost of emasculating the art itself. Such an attitude is part and parcel of a view of literature as a series of discrete aesthetic organizations to be valued solely for richness of texture and internal coherence of organization. Whatever is dangerous, radical, and *active* in Lawrence is thus brought under the control of an aesthetic appreciation of the work.

---

[2] Eliseo Vivas, *D. H. Lawrence: The Failure and the Triumph of Art* (Evanston: Northwestern University Press, 1960), p. 136.

This view involves a curious disregard of at least a century and a half of literary history. Ever since romanticism, imaginative literature has had the highest ambitions. Despising the progress of science and lamenting the decline of religion, the romantic poet conceived of himself as the supreme embodiment of the human spirit. Blake's passionate faith in the capacity of the imagination to construct a world,[3] Wordsworth's *Prelude* in which for the first time the poet *as* poet is hero,[4] Shelley's dictum that the poet is the unacknowledged legislator of the world:[5] these are major evidences of a new atmosphere in which poetic creation is taking place. In France the evidences are Flaubert's fanatical dedication to his art, Baudelaire's sense of the symbol (as used by the artist) as the means by which man penetrates the temple of nature, and Mallarmé's ambition to produce an *oeuvre pure*, which would give the quintessence of the experience of the world, purging through a kind of poetical alchemy all its dross, and make subsequent literature in a sense supererogatory.[6] Flaubert, Baudelaire, and Mallarmé are not the exact analogues of the English romantics,[7] but despite the differences between them both groups of writers wrote in a common atmosphere of belief in the supreme importance of the artistic imagina-

---

[3] See William Blake, "There Is No Natural Religion," in *The Portable Blake*, selected and arranged with an Introduction by Alfred Kazin (New York: Viking Press, 1946), pp. 77–78.

[4] "Tintern Abbey" and "The Immortality Ode" represent on a lesser scale the same intention.

[5] Percy Bysshe Shelley, "A Defence of Poetry," in *Essays and Letters*, ed. with an Introduction by Ernst Rhys (Garden City, N.Y.: Garden City Publishing Co., 1943), p. 41.

[6] See C. M. Bowra, *The Heritage of Symbolism* (London: Macmillan & Co., Ltd., 1947), pp. 1–16. Joyce's wish (it was also Blake's) that his readers devote their lifetimes to the understanding of his work reflects a similar ambition for *Ulysses* and *Finnegans Wake* (see Alfred Kazin, Introduction to *The Portable Blake*, p. 49).

[7] The exact analogues of the French writers are Pater and Wilde.

tion. One has only to compare the following passages from Coleridge and Mallarmé in order to be assured of their commonly held view of the creative and active function of poetry.

> Could I revive within me
> Her symphony and song,
> To such a deep delight 'twould win me,
> That with music loud and long
> I would build that dome in air,
> That sunny dome; those caves of ice!

> Une agitation solennelle par l'air
> De paroles, pourpre ivre et grand calice clair.[8]

Though they advocated a self-contained "pure aesthetic experience," the aesthetic writers also had a keen sense of the high importance of art and of its world-changing character. When Edmund Wilson rejected Eliot's view—the legacy of symbolism according to Wilson—"that a poet cannot be an original thinker and that it is not possible for a poet to be a completely successful artist and yet persuade us to accept his ideas at the same time,"[9] he could have invoked the symbolists to prove his point.

As I have pointed out, Lawrence has no sympathy with the aesthetic doctrines of Flaubert and the symbolists. Wherever he finds a passion for form, a value placed on art for its own sake, he senses an animus against life. Nothing repelled Lawrence more than the invidious disinctions made by aesthetic writers between art and life, typified by the outburst of the hero of Villiers' *Axel:* "Live? Our servants will do that for us."[10] Lawrence's conception of the right relationship between life and art is analogous to his conception of the right relationship between the passions and morality: life and art,

---

[8] I owe the comparison to Bowra, *The Heritage of Symbolism*, p. 219.

[9] Edmund Wilson, *Axel's Castle* (New York: Scribner & Sons, 1931), p. 119.

[10] Quoted in Bowra, *The Heritage of Symbolism*, p. 13.

the passions and morality, should be continuous with each other. But if Lawrence is unsympathetic to aestheticism, his work is filled with the high ambitions which romanticism conceived for literature. His work is intended to become an action in the world, that is, to achieve a radical revision of fundamental attitudes and feelings. This is his prophetic or moral character as an artist. Karl Jaspers' comment on the nature of prophecy, or "forecast" as he calls it, is illuminating.

> . . . A forecast . . . is the speculation of a man who wants to do something. He does not keep his eyes fixed on what will inevitably happen, but on what may happen; and he tries to make the future what he wants it to be. The future has become something that can be foreseen because it is modifiable by his own will.[11]

II

The successful action of art is never direct. When Lawrence exhorts his readers to make the necessary change in consciousness, either in his own voice or in the voice of one of his characters, the effect is strident and pathetic. The final pages of *Aaron's Rod* are a clear instance of Lawrence's direct, hortatory writing. There is hardly even the pretense of dramatization. Lilly pronounces "truths" with the authority of Lawrence, and Aaron is present merely as a sort of echo chamber.

> "We've got to accept the power motive, accept it in deep responsibility, do you understand me? It is a great life motive. It was the great dark power-urge which kept Egypt so intensely living for so many centuries. . . . Do you know what I mean?"
> "I don't know," said Aaron.

---

[11] *Man in the Modern Age*, trans. Eden and Cedar Paul (New York: Doubleday Anchor Books, 1957), p. 222.

"Take what you call love, for example. In the real way of
love, the positive aim is to make the other person—or persons—happy. It devotes itself to the other or to others. But
change the mode. Let the urge be the urge of power, . . ."[12]

Despite the differences among the various forms of imaginative literature, there is a common element which binds the
forms, the element that Lawrence calls art speech, the highest
speech of which man is capable. Art speech in its highest
form is symbolism. Lawrence would probably have sub-
scribed to Yeats's view of the symbol as expressed in the essays, *Symbolism in Painting* and *The Symbolism of Poetry*.

> All art that is not mere story-telling or mere portraiture
> is symbolic, and has the purpose of those symbolic talismans
> which mediaeval magicians made with complex colours and
> forms, and bade their patients ponder over daily, and guard
> with holy secrecy; for it entangles, in complex colours and
> forms, a part of the Divine essence.[13]

And he would also have agreed with what Yeats had to say
about the emotional qualities of the symbol, though he might
have objected to Yeats's "aesthetical" formulation:

> All sounds, all colours, all forms, either because of long
> association, evoke indefinable and yet precise emotions, or,
> as I prefer to think, call down among us certain disembodied
> powers, whose footsteps over our hearts we call emotions,
> and when sound, and colour, and form are in a musical rela-
> tion, a beautiful relation to one another, they become as it
> were one sound, one colour, one form, and evoke an emotion
> that is made out of their distinct evocations and yet is one
> emotion.[14]

Finally, however, Lawrence's conception of the symbol must
be radically distinguished from that of the symbolists and

---

[12] D. H. Lawrence, *Aaron's Rod*, Introduction by Richard Aldington (London: William Heinemann, Ltd., 1954), p. 288.

[13] Bowra, *The Heritage of Symbolism*, p. 185.   [14] *Ibid.*

their heirs. The kind of faith in art that symbolism presupposes Lawrence never possessed. There were few things he loathed more than the presumption of the aesthete or the symbolist that art is the triumph over life. Much as he loathed the actual world into which he was born, he could never have contrived the symbolic apparatus of Yeats's *A Vision* in order to re-create the world to his heart's desire.[15] The symbolical world designed to replace the actual world suffered from the mechanistic fallacy that life could be reduced to a system resembling a geometry. Ingenious (and on occasion evocative) as Yeats's system is, the impression of contrivance and artifice is much stronger than our sense of its reality.

Lawrence's symbolic imagination must also be distinguished from the allegorical conception of the symbol. As Lawrence himself remarked:

> You can't give a great symbol a "meaning." Symbols are organic units of consciousness with a life of their own, and you can never explain them away, because their value is dynamic, emotional, belonging to the sense-consciousness of the body and the soul, and not simply mental. An allegorical image has *meaning*. Mr. Facing-both-ways has a meaning. But I defy you to lay your finger on the full meaning of Janus, who is a symbol.[16]

Of course, to insist that a great symbol is essentially ineffable is to make the understanding of literature, not to say the critical discussion of it, almost impossible. And the proof of the difficulty that such a view proposes for critical discussion is illustrated by Lawrence's own essay on *Moby Dick* in *Studies in Classic American Literature*. Lawrence begins by stressing the irreducibility of the White Whale to any fixed

---

[15] See W. B. Yeats, *A Vision* (New York: Macmillan Co., 1956).

[16] D. H. Lawrence, *D. H. Lawrence: Selected Literary Criticism*, ed. Anthony Beal (New York: Viking Press, 1936), p. 157.

abstract meaning: "Of course, he's a symbol. Of what? I doubt if even Melville knew exactly. That's the best of it."[17] But such a view obviously is an obstacle to the understanding of the work, and Lawrence proceeds to assign a meaning to the whale: "What then is Moby Dick—he is the deepest blood being of the white race. . . . And he is hunted . . . by the maniacal fanaticism of our white mental consciousness."[18] Admittedly, the meaning that Lawrence assigns to Moby Dick is suggestive and consequently does not *fix* or compromise the meaning of the novel, but the contradiction in Lawrence's critical method suggests that he has far from settled the question of the symbol by attributing meaning to an allegorical image and ineffability to "a great symbol."

In *Apocalypse*, an interesting though little-known work, Lawrence conceives of the symbol more precisely and moreover in a manner which explains his own symbolic imagination. In a short chapter on image or symbolic consciousness, he distinguishes between modern and primitive consciousness. He criticizes modern image consciousness for its want of emotional value. "We always want a 'conclusion,' an end, we always want to come, in our mental processes, to a decision, a finality, a full stop."[19] To this kind of consciousness, Lawrence contrasts the mythical or symbolic consciousness of primitive man who "still thought of the heart or the liver as the seat of consciousness."[20]

> To them a thought was a completed state of feeling awareness, a cumulative feeling, a deepening thing, in which feeling deepened into feeling in consciousness till there was a sense of fullness. A completed thought was the plumbing of a depth like a whirlpool of emotion.

---

[17] P. 156.   [18] *Ibid.*, p. 173.

[19] D. H. Lawrence, *Apocalypse* (New York: Viking Press, 1932), p. 80.

[20] *Ibid.*

This should help us appreciate that the oracles were not supposed to say something that fitted plainly in the whole chain of circumstance. They were supposed to deliver a set of images or symbols of real dynamic value, which should set the emotional consciousness of the enquirer, as he pondered them, revolving more and more rapidly, till out of a state of intense emotional absorption the resolve at last formed; or, as we say, the decision was arrived at.[21]

The chapter in which Lawrence makes this distinction concludes, interestingly enough, with an attack on the modern political mind, "which lacks the courage to follow this intensive method of 'thought.' "[22]

What exactly is this intensive method of thought? And what is the connection between "the modern political mind" and the artistic imagination? At the conclusion of *The Birth of Tragedy*, Nietzsche has this to say about the nature of myth:

Without myth . . . every culture loses its healthy creative natural power: it is only a horizon encompassed with myths that rounds off to unity a social movement. It is only myth that frees all the powers of the imagination and of the Apollonian dream from their aimless wanderings. The mythical figures have to be the unnoticed omnipresent genii, under whose care the young soul grows to maturity, by the signs of which the man gives meaning to his life and struggles: and the state itself knows no more powerful unwritten law than the mythical foundation which vouches for its connection with religion and its growth from mythical ideas.[23]

The argument for myth is by now a familiar one. In social theorists like Sorel and Peguy, myth is the *sine qua non* of social change. And in the literary productions of every great

[21] *Ibid.*, p. 81.

[22] *Ibid.*, p. 82.

[23] Friedrich Nietzsche, *The Birth of Tragedy*, trans. Clifton P. Fadiman, in *The Philosophy of Nietzsche* (New York: Modern Library, 1950), p. 1077.

poet since the romantic period, the search for a mythology has been at the very heart of the poetic enterprise. Whatever danger attends our use of myth as a category of value, myth has become precisely that for the modern world. If it can be used as an instrument of repression, myth can also be used as a way out of the *cul de sac* of a moribund way of life. And it is the latter use of the myth that is one of the chief glories of the modern poetic imagination.

Myth, which is prior to person and society, is the common human fate from which there is no escape and of which there is finally no understanding; it is the fundamental reality that is presupposed by the recurrent patterns that manifest themselves in the actions of men in the world and in books. Myth then is anterior to the artistic and the political act. Modern self-consciousness about myth reflects the feeling that the community of symbol and idea which was readily available to artists of previous times has disintegrated. The modern person no longer has the assurance "which belongs to [myth and] ritual alone: that what is done below is done above, what is done here and now is done forever, what is repeated in time subsists unbroken in eternity."[24]

When we speak of the modern poet as being in "quest of myth" or as the creator of a private mythology, we tend to forget that myth is a product of the social or collective imagination and that the genuine myth-maker is a poet who has for a moment become the vehicle through which the archetypal or collective consciousness expresses itself. For us the personal signature of the myth-maker is an irrelevancy. Personality becomes relevant only in a work of art. The felt lack of a vital communal myth in the modern world is the generic problem of the modern poet—as it is of the political and so-

[24] Leslie A. Fiedler, *No! In Thunder: Essays on Myth and Literature* (Boston: Beacon Press, 1960), p. 300.

cial thinker, and it is reflected in the radical condition of privacy in which the modern poetic imagination has developed. "The isolation of the artist" in the modern world is only one manifestation of the disintegration of mythical consciousness. Lawrence is distinguished from the modern poets by his energetic refusal to accept the isolation that the modern world imposes not only on the artist, but on every man.

> Every *citizen* is a unit of worldly power. A *man* may wish to be a pure Christian and a pure individual. But since he *must* be a member of some political state, or nation, he is forced to be a unit of worldly power.[25]

The theme of *Apocalypse* is the wholeness of the cosmos and the illusoriness of "individualism": "What we want is to destroy our false, inorganic connections, especially those related to money, and reestablish the living organic connections, with the cosmos, the sun and earth, with mankind and nation and family."[26] Lawrence repudiates modern individualism in behalf of a higher idea of the fulfilment of the individual in the cosmic order.

Lawrence's effort then is not simply the making or the finding of a myth which will create a new unity in the cosmos. It is much more fundamental than that. Lawrence attempts nothing less than the reawakening of the faculty of mythical consciousness, which has degenerated into intellectual consciousness. He wants to reverse the evolution of mythos into logos. His task is far greater than the oracle's, for the oracle has only to be sure of his inspiration, whereas Lawrence has set for himself the task of reawakening the mythical consciousness of modern man so that the oracular authority, the authority of gods and demons, will once more be accepted. When Lawrence delivers "a set of images or

---

[25] *Apocalypse*, p. 194. [26] *Ibid.*, p. 200.

symbols of real dynamic value," he cannot, as does the oracle, presuppose a responsive "inquirer." The possibility that the symbol will be opaque is great, for the bond that existed between the oracle and the inquirer does not exist between Lawrence and his reader. If he is to succeed, he must not only deliver the dynamic symbols, but through the agency of art and rhetoric re-educate the consciousness of his readers so that the symbols will move them. In *Apocalypse* Lawrence evokes the world in which mythical consciousness was the dominant mode:

> the very ancient world was entirely religious and godless. While men still lived in close physical unison, like flocks of birds on the wing, in a close physical oneness, an ancient tribal unison in which the individual was hardly separated out, then the cosmos, the whole cosmos was alive and in contact with the flesh of man, there was no room for the intrusion of the god idea. It was not until the individual began to feel separated off, not until he fell into awareness of himself, and hence into apartness; not mythologically, till he ate of the Tree of Knowledge instead of the Tree of Life, and knew himself *apart* and separate, that the conception of a God arose, to intervene between man and the cosmos. The very oldest notions of man are purely religious, and there is no notion of any sort of god or gods. God and gods enter when man has "fallen" into a sense of separateness and loneliness.[27]

Lawrence's travel books on Mexico and Etruscan places are superb attempts to recover this world. For the American Indians there is "never the distinction between God and God's creation"; "creation is a great flood, forever flowing in lovely and terrible waves."[28] The Indians believe in the brotherhood of all living things. "The snakes are the Indians' brothers,

---

[27] *Ibid.*, pp. 159–60.

[28] *Mornings in Mexico* (London: William Heinemann, Ltd., 1956), p. 51.

and the Indians are the snakes' brothers."[29] All belong to the
great flood of creation. Everywhere among the Indians, Lawrence finds evidence of unity in the presence of divinity. In
the ceremonial dance there is none of "the hardness of repre-
sentation," of assuming a role, of representing something
else. "It is a soft, subtle *being* something."[30] Neither is there
spectacle and spectator. Everyone participates "in the home-
ward pulling of the blood as the feet fall in the soft, heavy
rhythm, endlessly . . . falling back from the mind, from sight
and speech and knowing, back to the great central source
where there is rest and unspeakable renewal."[31] On the
painted tombs of Tarquinia, Lawrence reads a similar story
about the extinct Etruscan civilization. The Etruscans, too,
had a cosmic religion in which "their gods were not beings,
but symbols of elemental powers."[32] And, as with Indian
civilization, the diversity of the cosmos subsisted in "a form
of [vital] unison."

> All things emerged from the blood-stream, and the blood-
> relation, however complex and contradictory it might be-
> come, was never interrupted or forgotten. There were dif-
> ferent currents in the blood-stream, and some always clashed:
> bird and serpent, lion and deer, leopard and lamb. Yet the
> very clash was a form of unison, as we see in the lion which
> also has a goat's head.[33]

In the light of our knowledge of Lawrence's ambition to
recover or reawaken mythical consciousness in the modern
world, it would be instructive to observe this ambition as
it is realized in two of Lawrence's most remarkable tales.

---

[29] *Ibid.*, p. 64.

[30] *Ibid.*, p. 50.

[31] *Ibid.*, p. 49.

[32] *Etruscan Places* (London: William Heinemann, Ltd., 1956), p. 66.

[33] *Ibid.*, p. 67.

III

In both *The Fox* and *St. Mawr* there are creatures from the subhuman world which have the kind of symbolic dimension that Lawrence attributes to "the great symbol"—that is, the full symbolic import of the fox or the horse is not fixed from the outset. It is realized as the tale unfolds in the complex relationships between the creatures and the human characters of the tales; and it is realized in a way which defies the abstract formulation that the allegorical symbol yields.

The action of *The Fox* takes place on a chicken farm owned and run by two young women, Banford and March. The fact, immediately given in the opening sentence of the tale, that they are known by their surnames,[34] their insistence on doing all the work themselves, March's resemblance to "some graceful, loose-balanced young man"[35] when she worked outdoors—all help to create an atmosphere of strangeness and perverseness. Life on the farm is difficult and resistant, and the increasing irritations of the life, particularly in March's experience of it, suggest that something is being denied, an indication of which is given in the qualification of the description of March's masculine movements in her work.

> But her face was not a man's face ever. The wisps of her crisp dark hair blew about her as she stopped, her eyes were big and wide and dark, when she looked up again, strange, startled, shy and sardonic at once.[36]

Into the life of chicken-farming comes its natural enemy, the fox. The first encounter between March and the fox gen-

---

[34] It was the custom of "emancipated" women of the twenties to call one another by their surnames. See John Montgomery, *The Twenties: An Informal Social History* (New York: Macmillan Co., 1957), p. 161.

[35] D. H. Lawrence, *The Fox*, in *The Short Novels*, Introduction by Richard Aldington (2 vols.; London: William Heinemann, Ltd.), I, 4.

[36] *Ibid.*

erates that peculiar symbolic atmosphere which is the hall-mark of Lawrence's art.

> She lowered her eyes, and suddenly saw the fox. He was looking up at her, his chin was pressed down, and his eyes were looking up. They met her eyes. And he knew her. She was spellbound—she knew he knew her. So he looked into her eyes, and her soul failed her. He knew her, he was not daunted.
>
> She put her gun to her shoulder, but even then pursed her mouth, knowing it was nonsense to pretend to fire. So she began to walk slowly after him, in the direction he had gone, slowly, pertinaciously. She expected to find him. In her heart she was determined to find him. What she would do when she saw him again she did not consider. But she was determined to find him. So she walked abstractedly about on the edge of the wood, with wide, vivid dark eyes, and faint flush in her cheeks. She did not think. In strange mindlessness she walked hither and thither.[37]

As the tale unfolds, the fox occupies an ever increasing importance in March's awareness—"it was the fox that dominated unconsciousness, possessed the blank part of her musing"[38]—and with the appearance of Henry, the young man, a sudden identification is made between his sharp bright curiosity and the fox.

> Whether it was the thrusting forward of his head, or the glisten of fine whitish hairs on the ruddy cheek-bones, or the bright, keen eyes, that can never be said: but the boy was to her the fox, and she could not see him otherwise.[39]

With the appearance of the young man, all the elements in the dramatic situation are present. Henry disrupts the precarious order of the household, as the fox threatens to disrupt the chicken farm, by exercising a strange spell on March. March's awareness of Henry as the fox deepens, and with

---

[37] *Ibid.*, pp. 6–7.   [38] *Ibid.*, p. 8.   [39] *Ibid.*, p. 11.

this deepening awareness the passion and fear increase. One night she dreams that she hears the fox singing and that she sees him "very yellow and bright, like corn." But when she stretches out her hand to him, he bites her wrist and his tail sweeps across her face and "burns her mouth with great pain."[40] The tale records the slow overcoming of March's resistant will—the agonizing surrender that she must make in her essential femaleness to Henry's maleness. She must overcome the fear of "the quality of his physical presence," which at the outset she finds "too penetrating, too hot."[41] The surrender occurs only with the murder of Banford, who, of course, represents March's connection with the old life, but even then the surrender is equivocal. March agrees to go off to America, and the tale ends on a mixed note of hope and despair.

[handwritten margin note: WRONG — THIS REFERS TO BANFORD]

The presence of the fox in the story is so intense and luminous that its allegorical meaning—the fox, we might say, is a symbol of natural sexual vitalities—gives no indication of the actual power of that presence. The recurrent experience that March has of the fox, either directly or through Henry, resembles the kind of experience that is found in the accounts of mythical cultures by anthropologists. Ernst Cassirer in his admirable volume on *Language and Myth* cites one such account and comments on it.

> "To the mind of the Evé, the moment in which an object or any striking attributes of it enter into any noticeable relation, pleasant or unpleasant, with the life and spirit of man, that moment a Trõ is born in his consciousness." It is as though the isolated occurrence of an impression, its separation from the totality of ordinary, commonplace experience, produced not only a tremendous intensification, but also the highest degree of *condensation*, and as though by virtue of this condensa-

---

[40] *Ibid.*, p. 16.   [41] *Ibid.*, p. 25.

tion the objective form of the god were created so that it veritably burst forth from the experience.[42]

In relating the phenomenon of the momentary god (the Trõ) to language itself, Cassirer stresses the subjective and creative function of language: "Whatever appears important for our wishing and willing, our hope and anxiety, for acting and doing: that and only that receives the stamp of verbal meaning."[43] Cassirer's statement about language applies to mythical consciousness itself:

> For mythical formulation as such cannot be understood and appreciated simply by determining the *object* on which it is immediately and originally centered. It is, and remains, the same miracle of the spirit and the same mystery, no matter whether it covers this or that realistic matter, whether it deals with the interpretation and articulation of psychical processes or physical things, and in the latter case, just what particular things these may be.[44]

The resemblance between mythical consciousness and the mode by which March apprehends the fox is, of course, not fortuitous. In employing this mode of awareness as a major element of his fiction, Lawrence's relationship with the reader reproduces in a sense the relationship between the fox and March, that is, to the extent that the tale is successful. Like the action of the fox on March's consciousness, the tale itself is that high degree of condensation of experience by virtue of which a sort of divine presence "veritably burst(s) forth from the experience." And March's response to the vividness and menace of the experience is, from this point of view, a surrogate for the reader's response to the tale. Even Henry, who seemed free of March's scruples throughout the tale,

---

[42] Ernst Cassirer, *Language and Myth* (New York and London: Harper & Bros., 1946), p. 34.

[43] *Ibid.*, p. 37.   [44] *Ibid.*, p. 11.

has "pain in his voice" as he wistfully anticipates the new
life across the sea: "If only we could go soon."[45] The fox
with his bright, sharp, impersonal eyes and his bushy, flame-
like tail has exacted a terrible price. Is Henry's pain, one
wonders, the beginning of a gnawing guilt? The unresolved
ending of the story corresponds to the irresolution of the
reader's consciousness, when presented with the splendor and
terror of a new life possibility. In conceiving the tale, Lawrence has performed "the miracle of spirit" which enables the
mind to apprehend nature as a field charged with divinity. And
he has magnified the miracle by performing it in a time when
the faculty for performing the miracle has all but withered
away.

Lawrence writes out of the recognition that as man has become emancipated from mythical thinking, as his language,
thought, and art have become more conceptual and abstract,
the wealth and fulness of immediate experience have become
more remote from his life. The only recourse that man has in
such a situation is art expression, which, as Cassirer points
out, is the human activity that is most closely connected with
the mythopoeic faculty, though it "no longer [represents] a
life mythically bound and fettered."[46] Cassirer concludes
Language and Myth with an admirable summary of the change
that occurs in the epistemological character of artistic expression, when it has freed itself from the mythical round.

> Word and mythic image, which once confronted the hu-
> man mind as hard realistic powers, have now cast off all
> reality and effectuality; they have become a light bright
> ether in which the spirit can move without let or hindrance.
> This liberation is achieved not because the mind throws
> aside the sensuous forms of word and image, but in that it

---

[45] *The Fox*, in *The Short Novels*, I, 69.

[46] Cassirer, *Language and Myth*, p. 98.

uses them as *organs* of its own, and thereby recognizes them for what they really are: forms of its own self-revelation.[47]

One might quarrel with Cassirer's insistence on the illusory character of an art liberated from the mythical world. It is indeed the poet's "illusion" that the reality of the world dwells within his imagination. However, Cassirer redeems his argument by his recognition that the sensuous forms of word and image are forms of the mind's "own self-revelation." And here we have the essential action that the tale performs on the reader's consciousness. *The Fox* is a kind of parable of the mythopoeic faculty. The relationship between March and the fox is intended to awaken the reader's dormant faculty for mythical thinking—for apprehending the universe as alive with deity.

In *St. Mawr* there is explicit speculation on the nature of mythical consciousness and being. The world of *St. Mawr* is post–World War I, and it is constituted by "the international set." Lou Witt, the wilful heroine of the tale, is "American: Louisiana family, moved down to Texas."[48] She is uneasily, irritably married to a son of an English baronet, a young artist of the aesthetical variety. In the first few pages of the story the itineraries of their lives are briefly sketched. After an education in France, Lou "drifted from Paris to Palermo. Biarritz to Vienna and back via Munich to London, then down again to Rome. Only fleeting trips to America."[49] She met 'Rico in Rome, had a love affair with him on Capri; then there was a separation between them which took 'Rico to Australia and Lou back to America. The marriage occurred on their reunion in Europe, but it was doomed beforehand by

[47] *Ibid.*, p. 99.

[48] *St. Mawr*, in *The Short Novels*, I, 30.

[49] *Ibid.*

the atmosphere of nervous rootlessness in which they lived. Mrs. Witt, Lou's mother, is a sort of choric presence in the tale. Sharp in mind and will, she watches the progressive dissolution of the marriage "as it were from outside the fence, like a potent well-dressed demon, full of uncanny energy and a shattering sort of sense."[50] Mrs. Witt is an interesting and important character in her own right who undergoes significant experiences, but her role in the tale is essentially a subordinate one. She is primarily a witness to the profound change which her daughter experiences. And the most powerful agent of that change is the stallion St. Mawr.

The impact of St. Mawr on Lou's consciousness, like the impact of the fox on March's consciousness, cannot be reduced to a fixed symbolic meaning. In a discussion among Lou, 'Rico, and their friends there is an attempt to define the mysterious influence that the stallion exerts. The discussion concerns the god Pan and the forms that he has taken in human history. Cartwright describes Pan before "the anthropomorphic Greeks turned him into half a man."

> "I should say he was the god that is hidden in everything. In those days you saw the thing, you never saw the god in it: I mean in the tree or the fountain or the animal. If you ever saw the God instead of the thing, you died. If you saw it with the naked eye, that is. But in the night you might see the God. And you knew it was there."[51]

To Lou's question whether she might see Pan in St. Mawr, Cartwright replies: "Easily. In St. Mawr!"[52]

The association between the horse and Pan suggests an important difference between *The Fox* and *St. Mawr.* The fox fits Cassirer's definition of the momentary god that is presented to the mythical mind by the mind's sudden notice

---

[50] *Ibid.*, p. 6.   [51] *Ibid.*, p. 51.   [52] *Ibid.*

of novelty, charged with either menace or gratification. The fox is limited to March's immediate experience, and after the coming of Henry, the fox is apprehended almost exclusively as a presence in Henry. St. Mawr, however, despite the fact that he defines the human characters in the story in their relationship to him, has a life of his own, which has nothing to do with the human world. Lou loves him because "he stands where one can't get at him."[53] Unlike the fox, St. Mawr never becomes a presence *in* the human world. Lewis Morgan, the Welsh trainer, and the Indian Phoenix are in communion with St. Mawr, but that is because they have entered the other world, "silent, where each character is alone in its own aura of silence, the mystery of power."[54] St. Mawr is more than a symbolic presence in the story; he is, one can say without exaggeration, a character in his own right. Unless we confer the status of character on St. Mawr, it is impossible to understand the emotions that are attributed to him after he has thrown 'Rico during 'Rico's attempt to break him.

> He knew, and became silent again. And as he stood there a few yards away from her, his head lifted and wary, his body full of power and tension, his face slightly averted from her, she felt a great animal sadness come from him. A strange animal atmosphere of sadness, that was vague and disseminated through the air, and made her feel as though she breathed grief. She breathed it into her breast, as if it were a great sigh down the ages, that passed into her breast. And she felt a great woe: the woe of human unworthiness. The race of men judged in the consciousness of the animals they have subdued, and there found unworthy, ignoble.[55]

Lawrence's attempt to conceive a horse as a character recalls Swift's conception of the Houyhnhnms in *Gulliver's Travels.*

---

[53] *Ibid.*, p. 46.   [54] *Ibid.*, p. 92.   [55] *Ibid.*, p. 70.

Employing the traditional view of the horse as a noble animal, Swift contrasts the admirable Houyhnhnms to the Yahoos, Swift's version of man in his final degradation. There is more than a little of Swift's misanthropic animus in the descriptions of the human world in *St. Mawr*, and Lou's final acceptance of the "spirit" of Western America involves as complete a repudiation of the human world as Gulliver ever made.

> There's something else even that loves me and wants me. I can't tell you what it is. It's a spirit. And it's here on the ranch. It's here, in this landscape. It's something more real to me than men are, and it soothes me, and it holds me up.[56]

The difference between *Gulliver's Travels* and *St. Mawr*, however, is an important one. The dominant mood of *St. Mawr* is lyrical—Leavis calls it a dramatic poem[57]—and the horse is conceived with an unsatiric seriousness that contrasts him sharply with the Houyhnhnms. Magnificent as St. Mawr appears on numerous occasions, he is meant to suggest, to evoke, more than credulity will bear. It is for this reason that the human characters supplement St. Mawr's presence with speculations about the natural life. Lou's little speech to her mother about what it means to be "a real human animal" is an instance of this:

> "A pure animal man would be as lovely as a deer or a leopard, burning like a flame fed straight from underneath. And he'd be part of the unseen, like a mouse is, even. And he'd never cease to wonder, he'd breathe silence and unseen wonder, as the partridges do, running in the stubble. He'd be all the animals in turn, instead of one, fixed, automatic thing. . . ."[58]

---

[56] *Ibid.*, p. 146.

[57] See F. R. Leavis, *D. H. Lawrence: Novelist* (New York: Alfred A. Knopf, 1956), pp. 279–306.

[58] *St. Mawr*, in *The Short Novels*, II, 47.

The sudden evocation of the deer, the leopard, and the partridge defines the symbolic limitations of St. Mawr. He does not convey all that Lawrence wants him to convey. The brilliant, though troublesome, final portion of the tale in which a fierce landscape of western America is evoked and St. Mawr virtually forgotten is Lawrence's imagination breaking out of the symbolic limitations which the horse has imposed. The wild spirit in the landscape is the spirit that invests St. Mawr with life, but Lawrence's imagination finally needs greater freedom to communicate the full power of that spirit.

The wild spirit that descends on Lou and takes possession of her is an exclusive spirit. Lou alone of the little *human* world in which she has lived has the courage and the imagination to embrace it, for to embrace the spirit one must reject the world of men. The secret of the spirit of the landscape is its inhumanity, its terrible unconcern with, or even open hostility to, the lives of men.

> So it was, when you watched the vast and living landscape. The landscape lived, and lived as the world of gods, unsullied and unconcerned. The great circling landscape lived its own life, sumptuous and uncaring. Man did not exist for it.[59]

The man or woman who embraces the spirit gladly must suffer the consequences of its inhumanity. (Lou says, "It's something wild, that will hurt me sometimes and will wear me down sometimes.")[60] Yet to renounce this spirit is, in the Laurentian view, to renounce life itself. The spirit—as I intend to show in the succeeding chapters—is, according to

---

[59] *Ibid.*, p. 137.   [60] *Ibid.*, p. 146.

Lawrence, the creative source of every form of life. Whatever dangerous energies it contains, and danger attends every creative act, there can be no genuine *being* unless one avails oneself of the spirit. And it is the final recourse when the human world has lost its vitality. Despite the terrible and inhuman character of the natural spirit that Lawrence has invoked, it serves, or at least Lawrence means it to serve, the *human* interest. Again, as in *The Fox*, the relationship between the tale and the reader reproduces, so to speak, the relationship between the wild spirit and Lou Witt. The powerful dramatization of the fierce resistances of St. Mawr and the western landscape, even the inability of St. Mawr to contain the fiery spirit to which Lou finally submits, immediately involves the reader in a connection with the tale comparable to Lou's connection with both St. Mawr and the wild spirit.

The kind of symbolic action that is created in *The Fox* and *St. Mawr* is much more difficult to achieve in the novel. The symbolism in the novel must of necessity be more complex, as in the case of *Women in Love*, and the result is inevitably a kind of diffuseness which diminishes the impact on the reader's consciousness. When Lawrence tries to sustain a single effect in a long novel, as he does in the incantatory, ritualistic presentation of *The Rainbow*, the marvelous effects that he achieves are somewhat offset by the inevitable fatigue that the reader experiences and the consequent damning sense the reader has of the book's repetitiousness. The novel, with "its deep love of the fact and the empiric element in experience,"[61] and the spaciousness that it provides for that love to exhibit

---

[61] Mary McCarthy, "Fact in Fiction," *Partisan Review*, XVII (Summer, 1960), 440.

itself, is not an ideal opportunity for Lawrence. His imagination, like the poet's, tends toward the making of swift symbolic condensations of facts and experiences, which the novelist is generally at pains to present in careful detail. For this reason, Lawrence's shorter works, *The Fox*, *St. Mawr*, "The Woman Who Rode Away," *The Man Who Died*, etc., offer his symbolic and mythic imagination a greater opportunity to perform its prophetic-visionary role.

3

The Eternity of the Phenomenon

The freedom to conceive of nature normatively is one of the marks of the utopian imagination. Writers as different from one another as More, Bacon, Rabelais, Rousseau, Wordsworth, and Ruskin regarded nature as a normative basis for judgment. Though these writers had biases characteristic of their respective times, their naturalism represents a universal ingredient in utopian thinking. Even in Christian thought the natural depravity of man is counteracted by a natural innocence which can be recovered.[1] If one considers contemporary nightmare utopias in which the utopian impulse is satirized, one finds that the satirist has discovered within the so-called utopia its own antithesis. Huxley and Orwell do little more than show that utopia is after all not utopia; it has become anti-natural and anti-human.[2]

The utopian writer, rejecting the actual, imitates nature. The good life is life in or according to nature. The utopian thinker must have an adequate idea of nature if his utopianism

---

[1] See, for example, John Milton, *Paradise Lost* and *Paradise Regained*.

[2] See George Orwell, *1984* (New York: Harcourt, Brace, 1949), and Aldous Huxley, *Brave New World* (New York: Modern Library, 1946).

is to be cogent—especially if his idea of nature is not current, as is the case with Lawrence, or if the historical or contemporary forms of life do not illustrate it. The evidence that the utopian thinker delivers against the actual is that nature is not immanent in the actual, that actual life is a fabrication or falsification of natural life.[3]

In the modern period, the appeal to nature is a reaction against the experience of unreality and alienation. The ethic that the hero of a tale by Faulkner or Hemingway evolves draws its strength from the primitive or natural world. For instance, Faulkner's heroines (Dilsey of *The Sound and the Fury* or Lena Grove of *Light in August*) find their moral strength in the natural rhythms of life. We are presented with the paradoxical situation of a human world which no longer creates values and the presumably value-free natural world which provides the hero with an ethical code. (Even Conrad, with all his suspicions of the passional underside of human nature, honors the claims of nature. For Conrad as for Aeschylus, the furies have a place in the underground of civilized life. They are, so to speak, the Eumenides, beneficent spirits in the sense that every life must have access to the energies they embody.[4])

---

[3] Therefore Lawrence rejects the idea that the Oedipus complex defines the natural relationship between mother and son. Lawrence means to reconceive human *nature* so as to restore to it what it has lost in the present: its normative and moral character. Ironically, Lawrence's imagination of the male-female connection often seems determined by his own Oedipus complex. In a little known play by Lawrence, *The Widowing of Mrs. Holroyd* (New York: M. Kennerley, 1914), there is a peculiarly graphic instance of this. Mrs. Holroyd, a "voluptuous" woman with a dignity reminiscent of the mother in *Sons and Lovers*, is married to a collier dissolute in the manner of the father in *Sons and Lovers*. She recoils from him in disgust and finally hatred as she is courted by a man several years younger than she. This situation combines two central facts of Lawrence's life—his love of his mother and hatred for his father, and his marriage to an older woman who in certain ways was a surrogate for his mother. Lawrence never fully recognized the distance between his own life and his utopian imagination of the *natural* life of man.

[4] See, for example, Joseph Conrad, *The Secret Sharer.*

Camus' *The Stranger* is particularly instructive in its dramatization of the difficulties in making nature an ethical standard. Meursault, the hero, is happy for the first time when in jail he remembers the sound of the rippling water of the sea, its feel against his body, and the sun-gold face of his mistress Maria. For the first time in his life he has the sensation of his own identity, of the quiddity of his individual being. And when in the strange ending to the novel he desires only that his march to the guillotine be greeted by "howls of execration,"[5] he is again enjoying his new-found identity. The universe remains for Meursault as indifferent as it was on the day that he received news of the death of his mother, went to the movies, and began the affair with Maria, but the sudden reality of the sounds, sights, and feelings of his life becomes the occasion for a new sense of the meaningfulness of life. In a world in which human institutions are no longer objects of belief, the only recourse that man has against the growing sense of the meaninglessness of his life is his personal bodily experience. (This, to be sure, is a difficult recourse, since man, being what he is, suspects physical experience which is not sanctioned by the institutions that compose the human community.) The sun which lights up Maria's face also moves Meursault to commit murder. The contrast between the two moments illustrates the difficulty of proposing nature as the basis for a normative vision of life.

Eliseo Vivas in his study of Lawrence makes a case against the vitalist's claim for life and nature.

> In respect to morality the vitalist is, in one sense, on the same plane with the ascetic and life-denying values of, say, the Plato of the Phaedo. For it is not life but the good life that both are interested in. The difference lies in the values that

---

[5] Albert Camus, *The Stranger*, trans. Stuart Gilbert (New York: Vintage Books, 1956), p. 154.

the vitalist would prefer to see realized, as against those that
his opponent would.[6]

Vivas' *caveat*, valuable as it is, should not, however, deprive
us of the values implicit in the words life and nature. The difference does, indeed, apply to the values that the vitalist
would prefer to see realized, but the appeal to life and nature
implies values, which only a positivistic skepticism would refuse to recognize.

Nietzsche, too, had his suspicion of nature lovers: despite
his own celebrations of natural vitality, Nietzsche mistrusted
certain idealisms which are presumably based on nature.

> You desire to *live* "according to Nature"? Oh, you noble
> Stoics, what fraud of words! Imagine to yourselves a being
> like Nature, boundlessly extravagant, boundlessly indiffer-
> ent, without purpose or considerations, without pity or jus-
> tice, at once fruitful and barren and uncertain: imagine to
> yourself *indifference* as power—how *could* you live in ac-
> cordance with such indifference? To live—is not that just
> endeavoring to be otherwise than this nature? Is not living,
> valuing, preferring, being unjust, being limited, endeavoring
> to be different? And granted that your imperative, "Living
> according to Nature" means actually the same as "living ac-
> cording to life"—how could you do differently? . . . In
> your pride, you wish to dictate your morals and ideals to Na-
> ture, to Nature herself, and to incorporate them therein.[7]

With his characteristic acuity Nietzsche has seen an illicit
attempt to use nature as a justification for actions and attitudes that have nothing to do with nature. It is, however, the
opposite of Lawrence's intention "to dictate . . . morals and
ideals to nature." All of Lawrence's vigilance is directed

---

[6] *D. H. Lawrence: The Failure and the Triumph of Art* (Evanston: Northwestern University Press, 1960), p. 34.

[7] Friedrich Nietzsche, *Beyond Good and Evil*, trans. Helen Zimmern, in *The
Philosophy of Nietzsche* (New York: Modern Library, 1950), pp. 388–89.

against the easy and fatal appropriation of nature to the mechanisms of human life. Lawrence would have agreed with Rilke, a kindred spirit, when Rilke distinguishes the false ease of conventional life from the strenuous and courageous effort to live according to nature.

> People have (with the help of the conventions) oriented all their solutions towards the easy, and towards the lighter side of what is easy; but it is very clear that we must hold to what is difficult, everything alive holds to it, everything in Nature grows and defends itself in its own way and is characteristic out of itself, seeks at all costs to be so and against all opposition.[8]

Lawrence's (and Rilke's) view that man is radically estranged from nature and must recover his connection with it is, of course, as old as romanticism. In his historical analysis of the *bifurcation* that has occurred between man and the world since the Renaissance, Whitehead provides an insight into man's radical estrangement from natural life.[9] The philosophical distinctions between subject and object, between the secondary and primary qualities of an object, that are presupposed by modern science have divided the world into two kinds of reality, incommensurate with one another. The objective world, the world constituted by primary qualities, is the province of the cold abstractions of science, which has the powers of manipulation and prediction; the subjective world, the world constituted by secondary qualities, is the province of poetry, which has the powers of description and evocation. If science has failed to grasp the object whole, it is not because it is generically inadequate to the task. "The abstrac-

---

[8] Rainer Maria Rilke, *Letters to a Young Poet*, trans. M. D. Herter Norton (New York: W. W. Norton & Co., Inc., 1940), p. 53.

[9] See *Science and the Modern World*, in *Alfred North Whitehead: An Anthology*, ed. with an Introduction by F. S. C. Northrop and Mason W. Gross (New York: Macmillan Co., 1953), pp. 363–466.

tions of science are [not] irreformable,"[10] Whitehead insists. Science has suffered from the legacy of the seventeenth and eighteenth centuries, the legacy of abstractions which do not correspond to our experience of the world. When Whitehead exposes science to the criticism of poetry, he does not mean to show the generic limitations of the scientific enterprise; rather he means to instruct science in the new path it must take. The difference between Whitehead and the romantic poets, whom he so admires and for whom "the whole of nature is . . . involved in the tonality of the particular instance,"[11] is the difference between the disciplines from which they approach the same problem.

Whitehead's chapter on the romantic reaction in *Science and the Modern World* is, without dealing directly with Lawrence, an excellent introduction to the significance of Lawrence as a "nature poet." Whitehead begins the chapter by noting the perplexity "which haunts the modern world,"[12] arising from a felt "discrepancy between the materialistic mechanism of science and the moral intuitions, which are presupposed in the concrete affairs of life."[13] The division of the world into subject and object, secondary qualities and primary qualities, has not only distorted our picture of the world, but it has divested the natural world of value. According to Whitehead, "the romantic revival was a protest on behalf of the organic view of nature, and also a protest against the exclusion of value from the essence of matter of fact."[14] The aesthetic properties of nature, the "brooding, haunting" mystery of mountain, forest, and lake,[15] were for Wordsworth and Shelley immanent in nature rather than products of fancy. The romantic insistence on the *objectivity* of "the brood-

---

[10] *Ibid.*, p. 438.

[11] *Ibid.*, p. 439.

[12] *Ibid.*, p. 436.

[13] *Ibid.*, p. 435.

[14] *Ibid.*, p. 449.

[15] *Ibid.*, pp. 439, 447.

ing presence of the hills" was a kind of protest in anticipation of the division that was to arise in the nineteenth century between poetry and science, a protest, in other words, against the view that poetry is the domain of subjectivity and value and science the domain of objectivity and truth.

> Now it is emphatically not the case that Wordsworth hands over inorganic matter to the mercy of science, and concentrates on the faith that in the living organism there is some element that science cannot analyze. Of course, he recognizes, what no one doubts, that in some sense living things are different from lifeless things. But that is not his main point. It is the brooding presence of the hills which haunts him. His theme is nature *in solido*, that is to say, he dwells on that mysterious presence of surrounding things, which imposes itself on any separate element that we set up as an individual for its own sake. He always grasps the whole of nature as involved in the tonality of the particular instance. That is why he laughs with the daffodils, and finds in the primrose thoughts "too deep for tears."[16]

Whitehead's conception of organic being, derived from "the romantic reaction," presupposes value as a synonym of reality. " 'Value' is the word I use for the intrinsic reality of an event."[17] Value like reality is an end in itself. "Remembering the poetic rendering of our concrete experience, we see at once that the element of value, of being an end in itself, of being something which is for its own sake, must not be omitted in any account of an event as the most concrete actual something."[18] Thus Lawrence's repeated insistence on the unreality of the actual world in which he lived, e.g., the *nullity* that permeates Ursula's experience in *The Rainbow*, reflects his romantic organicist's view that there is no reality

---

[16] *Ibid.*, pp. 438–39.
[17] *Ibid.*, p. 448.   [18] *Ibid.*

without value, that where the glow is missing there is death and unreality.

To say that Whitehead's chapter on the romantic poets is an excellent introduction to Lawrence's conception of nature is not to suggest an identity between the conceptions of, say, Wordsworth and Lawrence. It is meant merely to make clear the animus of Lawrence's appeal to nature. Like those of the romantics and Whitehead, Lawrence's appeal to nature is part of an imaginative effort to overcome the *bifurcations* of the modern world.

In order to grasp Lawrence's unique view of nature, it is essential that it not be confused with the Wordsworthian view.[19] In a short piece included in *Phoenix* Lawrence has this to say about Wordsworth.

> And Pan keeps on being reborn, in all kinds of strange shapes. There he was, at the Renaissance. And in the eighteenth century he had quite a vogue. He gave rise to an "ism," and there were many pantheists, Wordsworth one of the first. They worshipped Nature in her sweet-and-pure aspect, her Lucy Gray aspect. . . .
>
> Lucy Gray, alas, was the form that William Wordsworth thought fit to give to the Great God Pan.[20]

This, of course, is malicious caricature, but like all of Lawrence's hostile caricatures of writers it has captured a moment in the writer's work from which Lawrence is distinguishing his own position.[21] Nature is not "sweet and pure" for Lawrence. Nor has it any of the sobriety that permits Words-

---

[19] I hesitate to use the word "romantic" here because of its lack of discrimination. I choose "Wordsworthian" because Wordsworth's vision of nature has come to stand for the romantic vision.

[20] "Pan in America," *Phoenix: The Posthumous Papers of D. H. Lawrence,* ed. with an Introduction by E. D. McDonald (New York: Viking Press, 1950), p. 23.

[21] The Lucy poems, of course, do not illustrate that moment.

worth's "philosophic mind."[22] Lawrence's nature is closer to the nature of Wordsworth's youth, "when the sounding cataract haunted [him] like a passion."[23] Again like the nature of Wordsworth's youth, it is often an avenging deity, a minister of terror as well as joy. Like the youthful Wordsworth, Lawrence valued the tough resistant quality of nature—its defiant otherness: "The hard, silent abidingness of rock, the surging resistance of a tree, the still evasion of a puma, the dogged earth-knowledge of the bear, the light alertness of the deer, the sky-prowling vision of the eagle."[24]

The terrible energy in nature which defies "the philosophic mind" is present in many of Lawrence's nature descriptions. The fierce, resistant landscapes of Australia and America in *Kangaroo* and *St. Mawr* yield none of the moral truths that Wordsworth discovered in the vernal impulses. Lawrence's celebration of nature in its aspect of fierceness and terror can best be grasped through Nietzsche's conception of Dionysian tragedy in *The Birth of Tragedy*.

In the Dionysian rites "the state and society, and, in general, the gulfs between man and man give way to an overwhelming feeling of unity leading back to the very heart of nature."[25] This feeling of unity belongs to mythical times, that is, before the emergence of Greek civilization in its Socratic form (a degenerate version of the Apollonian). "The Dionysian musician is, without any images, himself pure primordial pain and its primordial re-echoing."[26] In Nietzsche's account of the Dionysian state of being there is implicit the

---

[22] Wordsworth's phrase in "The Immortality Ode" (stanza x, l. 187) for the control his imagination has achieved in maturity after a weary life in the city and the return to nature.

[23] William Wordsworth, "Tintern Abbey," ll. 76–77.

[24] "Pan in America," *Phoenix*, p. 29.

[25] *The Philosophy of Nietzsche*, p. 983.   [26] *Ibid.*, p. 971.

reason for the emergence of Apollonian consciousness, that consciousness which attempts through the imposition of images and rational forms to separate man from nature and hence control it. In the Dionysian festival, "all of Nature's excess in joy, sorrow, and knowledge become audible, even in piercing shrieks."[27] And in his analysis of the Oedipus myth, Nietzsche sees Oedipus' terrible suffering as a punishment for his solution to the riddle of the sphinx. "It seems as if the myth were trying to whisper into our ears the fact that wisdom, especially Dionysian wisdom, is an unnatural abomination; that whoever, through his own knowledge, plunges nature into an abyss of annihilation, must also expect to experience the dissolution of nature in himself."[28]

It is an easy transition from Nietzsche's conception to the Freudian conception. The ego, in the Freudian view, is the Apollonian triumph over the powerful disintegrative Dionysian id. But there is a difference in emphasis in the two conceptions which is all-important and bears significantly on our understanding of Lawrence. Whereas in the opposition between id and ego Freud is usually on the side of the ego, Nietzsche in his conception of the opposition between the Dionysian and the Apollonian impulses tends to be the advocate of the Dionysian impulse. To be sure, Nietzsche desires a balance between the two.[29] But the animus of *The Birth of Tragedy* is directed against Socratism, that is, the kind of Apollonianism that relinquishes its recognition of "the Dionysian substratum" of existence and, by doing so, cheerfully and optimistically falsifies reality. Nietzsche is attacking form which

---

[27] *Ibid.*, p. 967.   [28] *Ibid.*, p. 965.

[29] "At the same time, just as much of this basis of all existence—the Dionysian substratum of the world—is allowed to enter into the consciousness of human beings, as can be surmounted again by the Apollonian transfiguring power, so that these two art-impulses are compelled to develop their powers in strictly mutual proportion, according to the law of eternal justice" (*ibid.*, p. 1087).

is opaque to the dangerous energies at large in existence. He would have agreed with Lawrence that "man cannot return to the primitive life, to live in tepees and hunt with bows and arrows,"[30] but he would also have agreed with Lawrence that man must in some sense "abandon his conquest of nature"[31] if he is to become accessible to the divine energies in the universe. In Nietzsche's terms, man must suffer, i.e., experience passion, if he is to become beautiful.[32] Unlike Nietzsche, however, Lawrence does not call the immersion in passional experience tragic. The Aristotelian view of tragedy, with its attention to the suffering and doom of the hero, created in Lawrence a mistrust of the tragic vision. But Lawrence's achievement, like the achievement of Nietzsche's Apollo, is the radiant glorification of "the eternity of the phenomenon."[33] Indeed, Lawrence's work is prefigured in Nietzsche's new understanding of tragic vision.

"The yea-saying to life, even to its strangest and most difficult problems: the will to life rejoicing at its own inexhaustibleness in the sacrifice of its highest types—" this is what I called Dionysian, this is what I meant as the bridge to the psychology of the tragic poet. "Not to relieve one's self of terror and pity, not to purge one's self of dangerous emotion by a vehement discharge (this was Aristotle's misunderstanding of it) but rather, far beyond pity and terror, to be the eternal joy of Becoming itself—that joy which also involves the joy of destruction."[34]

Ever aware that all things change, that all things must change if they are to live, Lawrence is also aware of the death present in change. The fear of death—Lawrence shares

[30] "Pan in America," *Phoenix*, p. 31.

[31] *Ibid.*

[32] Nietzsche, *The Birth of Tragedy*, in *The Philosophy of Nietzsche*, p. 1088.

[33] *Ibid.*, p. 1039.

[34] Nietzsche, *Ecce Homo*, in *The Philosophy of Nietzsche*, p. 868.

this view with Nietzsche and the existentialists—is ultimately a fear of life, that is, a fear of the risks of a Dionysian immersion in life. Death is the aim of a perfected life, and only those—and they are legion—who have what Rilke called unlived lines in their bodies have a horror of death.[35] The Laurentian hero has overcome the fear of death.

> I wish we were all like kindled bonfires on the edge of space, marking out the advance-posts. What is the aim of self-preservation, but to carry us right to the firing line; there what *is* is in contact with what is not. If many lives be lost by the way, it cannot be helped, nor if much suffering be entailed. I do not go out to war in the intention of avoiding all danger or discomfort: I go to fight for myself. Every step I move forward into being brings a newer, juster proportion into the world, gives me less need of storehouse and barn, allows me to leave all and to take what I want by the way, sure it will always be there; allows me in the end to fly the flag of myself, at the extreme tip of life.
>
> He who would save his life must lose it. But why should he go on and waste it? Certainly let him cast it upon the waters. Whence and how and whither it will return does not matter in terms of values. But like a poppy that has come to bud, when he reaches the shore, when he has traversed his known and come to the beach to meet the unknown, he must strip himself naked and plunge in: if he dare.[36]

What distinguishes this from the tragic sense of life is the tone—and, of course, what the tone signifies. There is no sense of the "waste of good" (A. C. Bradley's phrase for an important element in the tragic economy).[37] The individual life doesn't matter; the life within the individual ("the eternity of the phenomenon") is of supreme importance.

---

[35] See Norman O. Brown, *Life against Death* (Middletown, Conn.: Wesleyan University Press, 1959), p. 108.

[36] "Study of Thomas Hardy," *Phoenix*, pp. 409–10.

[37] A. C. Bradley, *Shakespearean Tragedy* (London: Macmillan & Co., Ltd., 1950), p. 37.

Lawrence's intense faith in the eternal vitality of the natural world transcends the momentary tragic regret over the fleeting quality of all the particular things that make up life. Death is for Lawrence the moment that precedes the new life that is coming into being. The death of the orderly in "The Prussian Officer," for instance, is hardly tragic in the Aristotelian sense, for it releases the boy from his death-in-life into a vivid symbolic relation with life itself.

> The bodies of the two men lay together, side by side, in mortuary, the one white and slender, but laid rigidly at rest, the other looking as if every moment it must rouse itself into life again, so young and unused from slumber.[38]

Lawrence's insistence on the impersonal vis-à-vis the personal presupposes this faith in the natural world. In his extraordinary sensitivity to the quality of life at any given moment, he looks beyond the individual embodiment of that life to its fresh successive embodiments. The following passage from *Sons and Lovers* in which Paul and Clara make love in an open field shows vividly how far Lawrence's vision carries us beyond the merely personal.

> It was all so much bigger than themselves that he was hushed. They had met, and included in their meeting the thrust of the manifold grass-stems, the cry of the pee-wit, the wheel of the stars. . . .
>
> To know their own nothingness, to know the tremendous living flood which carried them always, gave them the rest within themselves. If so great a magnificent power could overwhelm them, identify them altogether with itself, so that they were only grains in the tremendous heave that lifted every grassblade in its little height, and every tree, and every living thing, then why fret about themselves? They could let themselves be carried by life, and they felt a sort of peace

---

[38] D. H. Lawrence, "The Prussian Officer," in *The Complete Short Stories*, Introduction by Richard Aldington (3 vols.; London: William Heinemann, Ltd., 1957), I, 116.

each in the other. There was a verification which they had together. Nothing could nullify it, nothing could take it away; it was almost their belief in life.[39]

Impersonality is a virtue that has generally been attributed to writers like Flaubert and Joyce, for whom Lawrence showed a certain contempt. In Flaubert and Joyce the impersonality is largely a matter of technique: the technique that defeats the tendency toward an extreme *personal* investment in the fortunes of the protagonist. In Lawrence the impersonality is in the protagonist himself. Lawrence's self-projections (Birkin, Aaron, Somers, etc.) all give us in the quality of their beings that sense of *otherness* which keeps the novels from being maudlin pieces of self-indulgence. For Lawrence, impersonality involves that moment in the wilderness (metaphoric or actual) when the preservation instinct is transcended and the protagonist risks all for the experience of being alive.

The wonderful vividness of Lawrence's language wins our assent too easily, for it tends to make us overlook the difficulties which Lawrence's passion for extreme experience creates. When Lawrence speaks of "the aim of self-preservation" as that of carrying "us right to the firing line," he is defining the heroic moment in life in which man fulfils his highest nature. But this cannot be all of life. There is the daily life on the farm, in the factory, in the school, and at home, far behind the firing line: the life defined by what Lawrence calls "the dull spaces"[40] which it is the peculiar genius of the novelist to evoke. And this life is in opposition to the life of extreme experience. Moreover, the paradoxical conse-

---

[39] D. H. Lawrence, *Sons and Lovers*, Introduction by Richard Aldington (London: William Heinemann, Ltd., n.d.), pp. 414–15.

[40] D. H. Lawrence, Introduction to Giovanni Verga, *Cavalleria Rusticana and Other Stories*, trans. D. H. Lawrence (London: Jonathan Cape, 1928), p. 23.

quence of the extreme experiences that Lawrence desires is
that though they are motivated by a passion for self-fulfilment, they risk bringing about the annihilation or the disintegration of identity. This paradox produces in Lawrence
an ambivalent attitude toward these experiences. He both
wants the mindless connection with the living universe and
the separateness from a universe that in other moods he regards as demoniacally alive. The gods in Lawrence's universe are very much like Rilke's terrible angels—they are
simultaneously the objects of desire and fear. There is in
Lawrence the same ambivalence as in the second of the *Duino
Elegies:* "Every Angel is terrible. Still, though, alas! I invoke
you, almost deadly birds of the soul, knowing what you
are."[41] And the quiddity of those angels is expressed in the
first of the elegies:

> Who, if I cried, would hear me among the angelic orders?
> And even if one of them suddenly pressed me against his
> heart, I should fade in the strength of his stronger existence.
> For beauty's nothing but beginning of Terror we're still just
> able to bear, and why we adore it so is because it serenely
> disdains to destroy us. Each angel is terrible. And so I keep
> down my heart, and swallow the call-note of depth-dark
> sobbing.[42]

I cite Rilke because his affinity with Lawrence is remarkable. Rilke's passionate desire for transcendence, for
achieving being according to nature, was counterpointed
by a fear of actual physical disintegration.[43] As much as his
"heart" wanted to achieve new states of being and feeling, he

---

[41] Rainer Maria Rilke, "Second Elegy," *Duino Elegies,* German text with
introduction and commentary by J. B. Leishman and Stephen Spender (New
York: W. W. Norton & Co., 1939), ll. 1–3.

[42] "First Elegy," *ibid.,* ll. 1–10.

[43] Rainer Maria Rilke, *The Journal of My Other Self,* trans. M. D. Herter
Norton and John Linton (New York: W. W. Norton & Co., 1939), pp. 242–43.

had to suppress "the call note[s]" of his heart because of the fear that the angels who embody those states would "destroy" him. Lawrence's susceptibility to mystical or hallucinated states, and his paranoid vision of the world as a great enemy (his fear of what he calls in *Apocalypse* the destructive dragons of the universe),[44] generated a need in him to keep isolate and separate from the world.

Rilke's advantage over Lawrence is that he was constantly and acutely aware of the ambivalence and sought to embody it in his art. Lawrence's art is frequently a contradictory oscillation between the two poles. His vision of nature in its Dionysian aspect ("all of Nature's excess in joy and sorrow") often fails to register in his celebrations of nature. The terrible anti-human landscape of the Rockies in *St. Mawr*[45] or the shameless sensuality of Mellors and Connie in *Lady Chatterley's Lover* the night "the oldest shames" were burned out "in the most secret places"[46] are never fully reconciled to his other view of nature: "the rise of a poppy, then the after uplift of the bud, the shedding of the calyx and the spreading wide of the petals, the falling of the flower and the pride of the seed-head."[47]

Lawrence had a vision of nature in its excess of joy and sorrow, but he never wholly assimilated it to his imaginative economy. Indeed, the abstractness and euphemism of his rendering of some of the love scenes in *Women in Love* and *Lady Chatterley* suggest an inhibition of what might have been a fuller imaginative immersion in the Dionysian mystery.

---

[44] See *Apocalypse* (New York: Viking Press, 1932), pp. 144–45.

[45] See *St. Mawr*, in *The Short Novels*, II, 123–47.

[46] D. H. Lawrence, *Lady Chatterley's Lover* (third manuscript version, first published by Giuseppi Orioli, 1928), Introduction by Mark Schorer (New York: Grove Press, 1959), p. 297.

[47] D. H. Lawrence, "German Books: Thomas Mann," *Phoenix*, p. 313.

"The great hope" voiced by *The Birth of Tragedy* (as expressed by Nietzsche in *Ecce Homo*) brings Lawrence immediately to mind.

> Let us anticipate a century; let us assume the success of my onslaught on two thousand years of opposition to Nature, of the degradation of humanity. That new party of life-affirmers, which will take into its hands the greatest of all tasks, the elevation of mankind, as well as the relentless destruction of everything degenerate and parasitical, will establish *superabundance* of life on earth out of which the Dionysian state must rise once more.[48]

If Lawrence is one of the life-affirmers, his abiding commitment to the *principium individuationis*, the unmistakably English—and hence moral—character of his art, complicates the placing of Lawrence in the ranks of any party. Lawrence is caught between the impulse to present the Dionysian "radiance of the eternity of the phenomenon" and the impulse to present the Apollonian state of individuation, and his imaginative effort (far from a complete success) was to reconcile the two impulses, or rather to demonstrate that under the right conditions they were identical.

II

The discussion of *The Rainbow* in the first chapter suggests the significance of Lawrence's commitment to a Dionysian vision of reality in terms of his conception of character. His concern with what a character is "inhumanly, physiologically, materially"[49] may be expressed as a concern with the cosmic energy out of which individual character is created at the moment, so to speak, before individuation.

In his "Study of Thomas Hardy" Lawrence defines in an

---

[48] Nietzsche, *Ecce Homo*, in *The Philosophy of Nietzsche*, p. 869.
[49] See p. 21.

extended way the kind of radical disaffiliation from the traditional novel that his vision of reality involves. Hardy is the
occasion for Lawrence's meditations because he is the closest
to Lawrence in the English novel in his vivid apprehension
of man and nature as a living continuum. Lawrence categori-
cally states that of all the English novelists Hardy had the
deepest sensuous imagination, the strongest feeling for the
physical or the natural life.[50] That the moralities of the
novels are invariably Victorian in their mistrust of nature
and in their accommodation to, if not always respect for, the
conventional pieties creates some difficulty for Lawrence's
appreciation of Hardy. For Lawrence, it is another case of
the artist who has submitted his artistic instincts to an alien
metaphysic. But Lawrence wisely refuses to allow his bias
to compromise his vision of the essential power of Hardy's
sensuous imagination. Unlike Joseph Warren Beach, for
whom "Hardy sounds the death-knell of the old nature-
poetry,"[51] Lawrence with a creative artist's instinct is able
to discover Hardy's feeling for nature in statements and passages which are hostile to nature—as he does, for instance,
in his discussion of the evocation of Egdon Heath at the beginning of *The Return of the Native.*

Hardy's vision of the man-nature connection is in effect a
rejection of the old thoroughly humanized world of the novel,
the world of manners, morals, and money. In Hardy as in
Lawrence the focus is on the passional connection between a
man and a woman.

> One thing about them is that none of the heroes and
> heroines care very much for money, or immediate self-pres-
> ervation, and all of them are struggling very hard to come into
> being. What exactly the struggle into being consists in, is the

---

[50] See "Study of Thomas Hardy," *Phoenix*, p. 480.

[51] Joseph Warren Beach, *The Concept of Nature in Nineteenth Century English Poetry* (New York: Pageant Books, 1956), p. 521.

question. But most obviously, from the Wessex novels, the first and chiefest factor is the struggle into love and the struggle with love: by love meaning the love of man for a woman and a woman for a man. The *via media* to being, for man or woman, is love and love alone. Having achieved and accomplished love, then the man passes into the unknown. He has become himself, his tale is told. Of anything that is complete there is no more tale to tell. The tale is about becoming complete or about the failure to become complete.[52]

Lawrence is certainly Hardy's best critic, for he has seen with unmatched acuity what we can see more clearly in Lawrence's own work, the imagination reducing character or personality to its natural element, impatient with the social forms and facts with which the novel has been traditionally concerned. Hardy once wrote: "If all hearts were open and all desires known as they would be if people showed their souls—how many gaspings, sighings, clenched fists, knotted brows, broad grins, and red eyes would be seen in the marketplace."[53] And we can see the habit of Hardy's imagination to conceive of character in its natural aspect in *Tess of the d'Urbervilles*, in which Tess is so intensely imagined as a child of nature that the natural image itself sustains her through her misery.

> At last she got away, and did not stop in her retreat till she was in the thicket of pollard willows at the lower side of the barton, where she could be quite unseen. Here Tess flung herself down upon the rustling undergrowth of *spear grass*, as upon a bed, and remained crouching in palpitating misery broken by momentary *shoots of joy* which her fears about the ending could not altogether suppress.[54]

[52] "Study of Thomas Hardy," *Phoenix*, p. 410.

[53] Florence Emily Hardy, *The Later Years of Thomas Hardy* (New York: Macmillan Co., 1930), p. 133.

[54] Thomas Hardy, *Tess of the d'Urbervilles*, Introduction by Carl J. Weber (New York: Modern Library, 1951), p. 228. (Italics mine.)

The immediate impulse of Hardy's imagination is toward the emotional center, the life that is ordinarily unlived but that is *the life* of the character. Hardy, before Lawrence, brought to the surface of his novels the explosive natural life of a character which his daily social existence denies. Lawrence loves the explosive suddennesses in Hardy:

> It is urged against Thomas Hardy's characters that they do unreasonable things—quite, quite unreasonable things. They are always going off unexpectedly and doing something that no one would do. That is quite true, and the charge is amusing. These people of Wessex are always bursting suddenly out of bud and taking wild flight into flower, always shooting suddenly out of a tight convention, a tight, hidebound cabbage state into something quite madly personal. It would be amusing to count the number of special licenses taken out in Hardy's books. Nowhere, except perhaps in Jude, is there the slightest development of personal action in the characters: it is all explosive. . . . [They] explode out of the convention. They are people each with a real, vital, potential self, even the apparently wishy-washy heroines of the earlier books, and this self suddenly bursts the shell of manner and convention and commonplace opinion, and acts independently, absurdly, without self-knowledge or acquiescence.[55]

Lawrence's discussion of Hardy goes beyond mere appreciation or sympathy. The metaphysic of the Hardy tale—not the metaphysic of the artist, whom Lawrence regards as a liar—is conceived in the language of the Old Testament, but its spirit is akin to the Dionysian wisdom which is the essence of Nietzsche's conception of tragedy.

> Always he must start from the earth, from the great source of the Law, and his people move in his landscape like tame animals wandering in the wild. The earth is a manifestation of the Father, of the Creator, who made us in the law. God still speaks aloud in his works, as to Job, so to Hardy, surpassing

---

[55] "Study of Thomas Hardy," *Phoenix*, p. 410.

human conception and the human law. "Dost thou know the balancings of the clouds, the wondrous works of him which is perfect in knowledge? How thy garments are warm, when he quieteth the earth by the south wind? Hast thou with him spread out the sky, which is strong?"[56]

Yet there is a qualification in the above passage that goes to the heart of Lawrence's ambiguous conception of Hardy and ultimately defines the difference between Lawrence and Hardy. Hardy's people "move . . . somewhat like tame animals." They are not possessed by a vision of the radiance of the eternity of the phenomenon, "surpassing human conception and human law." Their actions and their attitudes are for the most part defined by human law, and human law, a product of Apollonian consciousness, separates man from creation, "from the earth." It is for this reason that nature is seen ambiguously by Hardy as both ally and enemy: the source of the hero's energy and the force that will betray him. Lawrence differs from Hardy in that he cannot accept the vision of nature as betrayer. So he "rewrites" Hardy's novels: *The Return of the Native*, for instance.

The Return of the Native is Hardy's first "tragic and important novel."[57] The tragic power derives from the heath, "primitive, primal earth, where the instinctive life heaves up."[58] Lawrence, unlike Hardy, sees fecundity rather than barrenness in the heath. (It is typical of Lawrence to perceive a *vital* meaning in a novel beyond the novelist's conscious intention.)

> What matters, any more than the withering heath, the reddening berries, the seedy furze, and the dead fern of one autumn of Egdon? The Heath persists. Its body is strong and fecund, it will bear many more crops besides this.[59]

---

[56] *Ibid.*, p. 480.   [58] *Ibid.*

[57] *Ibid.*, p. 415.   [59] *Ibid.*

The characters of the novel have all been heaved up by the soil, "one year's accidental crop."[60] The phrase perfectly expresses Lawrence's superb contempt for the idea of self-preservation. What matters is the life of the moment, a character's vivid connection with the soil.

> Three people die and are taken back into the Heath; they mingle their strong earth again with its powerful soil, having been broken off at their stem. It is very good. Not Egdon is futile, sending forth life on the powerful heave of passion. It cannot be futile, for it is eternal. What is futile is the purpose of man.[61]

This is tragic affirmation; "the very good" suggests transcendence of tragic regret for the doomed individual. The tragedy, as Lawrence sees it, is one of Hardy's (and his characters') own making. The pain and evil come from the refusal of Hardy's people to stay connected with the soil, from the development of small, futile purposes divorced from the life out of which the character sprung. Clym's stay in Paris is an instance of this; even more revealing is his meretricious return to the soil:

> He came back to Egdon—what for? To reunite himself with the strong, free flow of life that rose out of Egdon as from a source? No—"to preach to the Egdon eremites that they might rise to a serene comprehensiveness without going through the process of enriching themselves." As if the Egdon eremites had not already far more serene comprehensiveness than ever he had himself, rooted as they were in the soil of all things.[62]

Clym returns not to work the soil, but to preach the moral idea of the community, the code that defines "the little fold of law and order."[63]

---

[60] *Ibid.*

[61] *Ibid.*

[62] *Ibid.*, p. 417.

[63] *Ibid.*, p. 419.

Tess of the d'Urbervilles illuminates perhaps more than Hardy's other novels the imaginative ethos in which both Hardy and Lawrence write. Lawrence is not as helpful here as he is in his other re-creations. It is more useful to regard the novel apart from Lawrence's refractory understanding of it.[64]

Tess is the last of the line of an honorable family. The Norman blood still runs in her veins. There is the suggestion of a taint or of the thinning of the blood connected with the decline of the family. Tess' father drinks and Tess, the earth child, is unduly susceptible to the moral idealism of Angel Clare: the roots being weakened, she must be nourished from another source. Yet Tess is the only one of the three principal characters who has a real connection with the earth.[65] Both Angel and Alec are estranged from the natural world. Angel's situation is complicated. By giving up his father's evangelicalism and taking on the new liberal, free-thinking philosophy, he has lost his connection with his family and unwittingly with the land itself. His pastoral idyl is profoundly false. He remains unconnected with the land, simply an external student of the ways of the pastoral community at Flintcomb. Neither does Alec have a genuine relationship to the land and its traditions. His family has adopted an old name. *Nouveau riche*, he is a man forever adopting different names. Through-

---

[64] See Dorothy Van Ghent, *The English Novel: Form and Function* (New York: Rinehart, 1953), pp. 195–209. I am indebted to Miss Van Ghent in my discussion of *Tess*.

[65] Tess is divided in her affections between two members of the opposite sex who embody principles diametrically opposed to each other: Angel Clare, the spiritual, and Alec, the sensual. This is a characteristic triangle in Hardy's fiction: *Jude the Obscure, The Return of the Native, The Woodlanders, Far from the Madding Crowd*, etc. One is reminded immediately of Lawrence's own preoccupation with the man or woman divided between two kinds of love; for example, Paul Morel in *Sons and Lovers* divided between his affection for the spiritual Miriam and his passion for the sensual Clara.

out the novel we have a sense of the shabby theatricality of his disguises; we see in him the man who makes a false claim to tradition.

Implicit in the character of Tess is the proper relation between man and nature, a relation already confused and suffering in Tess. But she alone is at moments vitally connected with the pastoral community. The decline of her family suggests the antithetic tendency in her, that she, like Angel, is in danger of losing her connection with nature. The moral chaos of nature is its failure to find a vital communal form through which to express itself. Nature is no longer bound in a system of communal pieties: it is becoming abstract and explosive. The novel ends with an explosion of violence in which Tess for a moment realizes herself and carries Angel on the wave of her realization.[66] The natural life then is at once a danger and an opportunity. Hardy writes his novels with an acute sense of danger, though there is still within him a lingering fascination with the opportunity. For Lawrence, nature—the physical, bodily life of man—becomes primarily opportunity. All of Lawrence's imaginative career can be understood as a sustained effort to bind nature once again to the civilized life of man.

---

[66] We are reminded of the violent self-fulfilling actions of Lawrence's tales (e.g., *The Fox* and "The Prussian Officer").

The Greater Life
of the Body

To-day, as always, art must, willy-nilly, make Transcendence perceptible, doing so at all times in the form which arouses contemporary faith. It may well be that the moment draws near when art will once again tell man what his God is and what he himself is. So long as we (as if this were not yet taking place) have to contemplate the tragedy of man, the sheen of true being, in the forms of a long-past world— not because the old art was a better art, but because as yet we have no truth of our own—though we do indeed participate in the genuine labours of our contemporaries as our situation, still we do it with the consciousness that we are failing to grasp our world.[1]

Few modern writers fit Jaspers' characterization of the religious task of art as well as does Lawrence. Yet, curiously enough, on at least one occasion Lawrence himself regarded art and religion as contradictory human activities. For Lawrence, and I cite this passage once again, "the artistic effort is the effort of utterance, the supreme effort of expressing knowledge, that which has been once, that which was enacted, where the two wills met and left their result, complete

---

[1] Karl Jaspers, *Man in the Modern Age*, trans. Eden and Cedar Paul (New York: Doubleday Anchor Books, 1957), pp. 141–42.

for the moment."[2] To this Lawrence contrasts the religious effort, "the portrayal or symbolizing of the eternal union of the two wills, according to aspiration."[3] If Lawrence's art is religious, then the art is a contradiction in terms according to the contrast he makes here. Lawrence's difficulty is to reconcile his impulse toward transcendence (the achieving of a new relation to the cosmos, to *otherness*) with the obligation of every artist to present reality which has already been enacted and is recognizable. We have already seen in the previous chapters how in extending the frontiers of the novel, Lawrence dealt with a new kind of reality or fact. The success of Lawrence's art depends on his fidelity to this reality; the failure occurs when the imagination in its desire to achieve transcendence wilfully ignores the resistances of the world in which it has its life. The problem has been posed in a different context by Jean Paul Sartre.

> In particular will freedom by taking itself for an end escape all *situation?* Or on the contrary, will it remain situated? Or will it situate itself so much the more precisely and the more individually as it projects further in anguish as a conditioned freedom and accepts more fully its responsibility as an existent by whom the world comes into being.[4]

I invoke the existentialists, in the one case a Christian and in the other an atheist, at the outset of my discussion of the religious theme in Lawrence's work, because the issues of freedom, transcendence, and reality, which are among the essential religious issues, have been treated with an unmatched seriousness by the existentialist philosophers. The existen-

---

[2] "Study of Thomas Hardy," *Phoenix: The Posthumous Papers of D. H. Lawrence* (New York: Viking Press, 1950), p. 447.

[3] *Ibid.*

[4] Jean Paul Sartre, *Existentialism and the Human Emotions,* trans. Dr. Bernard Frechtman and Hazel E. Barnes (New York: Philosophical Library, 1957), p. 96.

tialists are not concerned with transcendence as a matter of doctrine to be incorporated into an institutional conception of religion. They are concerned with transcendence as *experience*. If Jaspers calls himself a Christian, it is not as a consequence of a deduction from the sacred texts or a traditional commitment to the Church; it is rather the result of an experiential struggle toward transcendence. This is the only genuine religious possibility for man in the modern world. As Jaspers himself has remarked:

> man, torn from the sheltering substantiality of stable conditions and cast into the apparatus of mass-life, deprived of his faith by the loss of his religion, is devoting more decisive thought to the nature of his own being. Thus it is that there have arisen the typical philosophical ideas adequate to our own epoch. No longer does the revealed Deity upon whom all is dependent come first, and no longer the world that exists around us; what comes first is man, who, however, cannot make terms with himself as being, but strives to transcend himself.[5]

The above passage is an accurate description of the situation in which Lawrence finds himself as a religious artist. Though Lawrence's profoundly religious nature would have prevented him from identifying the historical moment in which he lived as did Nietzsche when he announced that God was dead,[6] Lawrence was acutely aware of the lack of a genuine relationship between man and God. "We have lost him!"[7] cries Lawrence in momentary despair, and in order to find him again, men must be reminded of the religious faculty with which they are endowed.

---

[5] Jaspers, *Man in the Modern Age*, p. 156.

[6] See Nietzsche, *Thus Spake Zarathustra*, in *The Philosophy of Nietzsche*, Introduction by Willard Huntingdon (New York: Modern Library, 1950), pp. 319–32.

[7] "On Being Religious," *Phoenix*, p. 727.

However, the loss of God is seen by Lawrence as a significant religious fact. Man is not to blame for it: Lawrence does not attribute to modern man a nihilistic will to deny God's existence.

> Man is only man. And even the Gods and the Great God go their way; stepping slowly, invisibly across the heavens of time and space, going somewhere, we know not where. They do not stand still. They go and go, till they pass below the horizon of man.
>
> It is not our fault. It is nobody's fault. It is the mysterious and sublime fashion of the Almighty, who travels too. At least, as far as we are concerned, He travels.[8]

Thus changefulness is not only an attribute of man; it is also an attribute of the gods. In the changefulness of the gods the universe is renewed. The momentary loss of God is then an opportunity for a new creative finding of him, or in the language of the existentialists, a new striving toward transcendence.

If the gods refuse to stand still and "pass below the horizon of man," then the forms of transcendence must vary from age to age. A recent tendency in the criticism of Lawrence to stress his kinship with Christianity has simply failed to represent truly his religious identity. There is, to be sure, some evidence for this view. Toward the end of his career Lawrence evinced an admiration for the pagan element in the Catholic Church and was even hopeful about the regeneration of Christianity as an active religious force.[9] Moreover, Lawrence's attraction to the figure of Jesus was deep and abiding, and *The Man Who Died*, despite its elements of parody and satire, is a significant and (in certain ways) rever-

---

[8] *Ibid.*

[9] See *The Later D. H. Lawrence*, selected by William York Tindall (New York: Alfred A. Knopf, 1959), pp. 391–93.

ent re-creation of the Christ story. Lawrence's affection for the resurrection idea alone would seem to provide a ground for asserting his kinship with Christianity. One critic suggests that Lawrence may have been working all alone toward a Christian view of things and calls Lawrence "almost a Christian."[10]

All this, of course, is to ignore the fact that the essential animus of his work is averse to Christianity. If he celebrates the resurrection, he reminds us in *Apocalypse* that the resurrection theme is prominent in pre-Christian religions. Indeed, Christianity involves the transcendence of the idea of resurrection. Man is to rise to a place in the eternal scheme of things never to rise again. For Lawrence the rhythm of death and rebirth is an eternal rhythm which can never be transcended so long as there is life. Lawrence consequently loathed the idea of immortality. Even more crucial to Lawrence's view of Christianity is his peculiar appropriation of the idea of the Holy Ghost. The Holy Ghost, according to Lawrence, is that capacity within man which "can scent the new tracts of the Great God across the Cosmos or Creation." It is not a Way or a Word; it is rather the eternal capacity in man to discover the Way and the Word at every moment of his quest. Lawrence writes:

> never did God or Jesus say there was only one way of salvation, for ever and ever. On the contrary, Jesus plainly indicated the changing of the way. And what is more, He indicated the only means to the finding of the right way.[11]

Lawrence appropriates the idea of the Holy Ghost precisely to free himself from a commitment to Christianity. He sepa-

---

[10] Mark Spilka, *The Love Ethic of D. H. Lawrence* (Bloomington: Indiana University Press, 1957), p. 217.

[11] *Phoenix: Posthumous Papers of D. H. Lawrence* (New York: Viking Press, 1950), p. 729.

rates Christ from Christianity, and it is this separation that has given him the freedom to pursue God in his own way.

There is scarcely a work by Lawrence that is not part of this quest for new paths to the ever changing God. In his "Study of Hardy" Lawrence made one of his most ambitious attempts to give doctrinal expression to his religious intention. He begins by disengaging the self from those restrictions that would prevent it from pursuing God. In his freewheeling manner, he attacks the suffragette movement, laws, work, the state, and money. These are interests that bind men to some fixed idea of their destiny. They betray their hopes by promising a salvation which they cannot give. Thus, for example, Lawrence repudiates the belief in the power of social law to improve the lot of man:

> law is a very, very clumsy and mechanical instrument, and we people are very, very delicate and subtle beings. Therefore I only ask that the law shall leave me alone as much as possible. I insist that no law shall have immediate power over me, either for my good or my ill. And I would wish that many laws be unmade, and no more laws made. Let there be a parliament of men and women for the careful and gradual unmaking of laws.[12]

Hardy, the occasion for "the study," is the English novelist in Lawrence's immediate past who had a sense of the depths of the self below the conventions by which men generally understand themselves. Moreover, Hardy is the first great English novelist whose conception of the male-female relationship is almost entirely disengaged from conventional moral considerations. The tentativeness and confusion in Hardy's treatment of men and women arise from his having entered hitherto unexplored territory. Hardy's uniqueness in this respect is essential in relation to Lawrence,

---

[12] "Study of Thomas Hardy," *Phoenix*, p. 405.

because the life beyond the conventional round in which new things are possible has its origins "in the impulse of the male upon the female, the female upon the male."[13] This, in Lawrence's view, is the source of religious life, as it is of all life, and Lawrence understands all the creative expressions of man, whether in art or religion, as different ways in which that impulse has manifested itself. "As in the flower, the pistil, female, is the center and swivel, the stamens, male, are closeclasping the bud, and the blossom is the great motion outwards into the unknown, so in man's life, the female is the swivel and center on which he turns closely."[14]

If the religious idea arises from the desire of the male for the female and the female for the male, every religious idea will have a masculine or feminine character. The Jewish idea of God, according to Lawrence, is a female conception.

> It was the God of the body, the rudimentary God of physical laws and physical functions. . . . His religion had become a physical morality, deep and fundamental, but entirely of one sort. Its living element was this scrupulous physical voluptuousness, wonderful and satisfying in large measure.[15]

Christ rose from "the suppressed male spirit in Judea." Unlike Job, who remained true to his "utter belief in the body," he rejected the "senses, sensation, sensuousness, these things which are incontrovertibly Me."[16] Though Christ claimed that he had come not to destroy the law but to fulfil it, he did in effect destroy the law by denying that life was in the body. Lawrence renders the meaning of the crucifixion in the following manner: "In the body ye must die, even as I died on the cross," says Christ, "that ye may have everlasting life."[17]

The essential opposition between the Christian idea and the Jewish idea Lawrence conceives, in the traditional man-

---

[13] *Ibid.*, p. 444. [15] *Ibid.*, p. 450.

[14] *Ibid.* [16] *Ibid.*, p. 452. [17] *Ibid.*, p. 467.

ner, as the opposition between law and love. Law is the law of
the body, the personal body that has arrogated to itself divinity. Love is the recognition of the limitations of the personal
self, the recognition that there are other selves that have different, even hostile, laws. "The final lesson" of Christianity
is "submission." "Christianity ends in submission, in recognizing and submitting to the law of the other person."[18] In
Lawrence's view, the conflict between law and love is not
a necessary one. Since fulfilment cannot occur completely
either in the spirit or in the flesh, both the spirit and the body
must be regarded as "Complementary Absolutes."

> Why, when the body fails me, must I adhere to the Law,
> and give it praise as the perfect Abstraction, like Raphael,
> announce it as an Absolute? Why must I be imprisoned with-
> in the flesh, like Michelangelo, till I stop the voice of my
> crying out, and be satisfied with a little where I want com-
> pleteness?
>
> And why, on the other hand, must I lose my life to save it?
> Why must I die, before I can be born again? Can I not be
> born again, save out of my own ashes, save in resurrection
> from the dead?
>
> It is time that man shall cease, first to live in the flesh, with
> joy, and then, unsatisfied, to renounce and to mortify the
> flesh, declaring that the Spirit alone exists, that Christ He
> is God.[19]

Spirit and flesh are somewhat misleading equivalents for
love and law. When Lawrence speaks of the sensuous mysteries, he is speaking of the spirit immanent in the flesh. In
other words, he is repudiating the separation that religion,
philosophy, and literature have traditionally made between
body and soul. He does mean, however, to distinguish between two different modes of being and consciousness, and

---

[18] *Ibid.*, p. 512.   [19] *Ibid.*, pp. 468–69.

his wish for a fusion or a reconciliation between them ignores his own insistence on other occasions that the two modes of being are radically and fiercely irreconcilable. Indeed, the speculative portions of the two travel books, *Mornings in Mexico* and *Twilight in Italy*, are largely occupied with making this point. In *Mornings in Mexico* the opposition is represented by the Indian and the white ways of consciousness.

> The Indian way of consciousness is different from and fatal to our way of consciousness. Our way of consciousness is different from and fatal to the Indian. . . . They are not even to be reconciled. There is no bridge, no canal of connection. . . .
>
> The consciousness of one branch of humanity is the annihilation of the consciousness of another branch.[20]

In *Twilight in Italy* the opposition is conceived in terms of the northern and the pagan races, the Father and the Son, the Dark and the Light, the tiger and the lamb.

> The consummation of man is two-fold, in the Self and in Selflessness. . . .
>
> But he must never confuse them. They are eternally separate. The lion shall never lie down with the lamb. The lion shall eternally devour the lamb, the lamb shall eternally be devoured.[21]

If, as Lawrence feels, self and selflessness, lion and lamb, law and love, are each "a great half-truth" about life, "the only thing you can do is to have a little Ghost inside you which sees both ways."[22] But the capacity to see both ways is not the same as reconciliation, for "one man can belong to one great way of consciousness only."[23] The unmistakable implication

---

[20] *Mornings in Mexico* (London: William Heinemann, Ltd., 1956), p. 46.

[21] D. H. Lawrence, *Twilight in Italy* (London: William Heinemann, Ltd., 1956), p. 46.

[22] *Mornings in Mexico*, p. 46.   [23] *Ibid.*

of Lawrence's somewhat elliptical expression is that a man may have the power to make a choice, and if the choice is made under the aegis of "the little Ghost," he will choose the way through which the greatest life is manifesting itself at the particular moment. "The little Ghost" in Lawrence chose the way of the body: the way of the law, of immanence.

The life of the body, as Lawrence conceives it, is anterior to the distinction between spirit and flesh. I cite once again the passage in *Apocalypse* in which, describing the religious consciousness of primitive man, Lawrence in effect defines the kind of consciousness he recaptured for his art.

> . . . the very ancient world was entirely godless and re-ligious. While men still lived in close physical unison, like flocks of birds on the wing, in close physical oneness, an an-cient tribal unison in which the individual was hardly sepa-rated out, then the whole cosmos was alike and in contact with the flesh of man, there was no room for the intrusion of the god idea. . . . The very oldest notions of man are *purely* re-ligious, and there is no notion of any sort of god or gods. God and gods enter when man has "fallen" into a sense of sepa-rateness and loneliness.[24]

Lawrence has performed the remarkable feat of preserving in his imagination the pre-cognitive sense of the mythical mind: the sense that all the bodies of the world, animate and inanimate, are living sacred selves bound to each other in a mysterious, incomprehensible flow.

One critic misses the force of Lawrence's distinction be-tween the two modes of consciousness when he says that the difference between the Laurentian idea and the Christian "is not ineradicable. Whether man receives the sacred flow of life which God has given him, and remains thankful for that, or whether man transcends his finite self, to participate in the

---

[24] *Apocalypse* (New York: Viking Press, 1936), pp. 159–60.

God-stuff, the ultimate effect is the same."[25] It is precisely Lawrence's point that this difference makes all the difference in the universe.

> To pretend that all is one stream is to cause chaos and nullity. To pretend to express one stream in terms of another, so as to identify the two, is false and sentimental.[26]

The idea of the immanence of divinity in the body is a powerful idea, and it keeps its power only if its meaning is not reduced to an idea which is really its opposite. To blur the distinction is to do what a great deal of the criticism of Lawrence has tried to do; it is to domesticate the tiger. Both the Laurentian idea and the Christian idea derive from a repudiation of the actual world and a desire to transcend it; we remain, however, with the essential question of the particular form which transcendence takes in Lawrence.

II

The history of man's quest for transcendence is based on the view that man is the image of God by virtue of his possession of soul or mind, and the body is the prison from which the soul or mind must gain its freedom in order to achieve communion with God. In Lawrence's view, the paradoxical consequence of this has been the diminution of the self. And the reason for this diminution lies in the very nature of consciousness.

The pernicious tendency of consciousness, according to Lawrence, is to divide the self in two. In a short essay "Individual Consciousness vs. Social Consciousness" Lawrence proposes the following paradox:

---

[25] Spilka, *The Love Ethic of D. H. Lawrence*, p. 217.

[26] *Mornings in Mexico*, p. 46.

> . . . the individual is only truly himself when he is uncon-
> scious of his own individuality, when he is unaware of his
> own isolation, when he is not split into objective and subjec-
> tive, when there is no *me or you*, no *me or it* in his conscious-
> ness, but the *me and you*, the *me and it* is a living continuum,
> as if all were connected by a living membrane.[27]

The split within the human psyche between subjective and
objective creates within the mind a radical sense of the limita-
tion of *me* and consequently forces the mind into a constant
awareness of what is beyond the *me*—the you or it. "The
awareness of 'you' or 'it' as something definitely limiting
'me,' this is social consciousness."[28] Lawrence has seen with
remarkable acuity how the overdeveloped self-consciousness
of modern man is simply the obverse expression of his worry
about the social world; it is the other side of his social consciousness. Lawrence finds evidence for this in modern
novels.

> The more one reads of modern novels, the more one
> realizes that, in this individualistic age, there are no individ-
> uals left. People, men, women, and children are *not* thinking
> their own thoughts, they are not feeling their own feelings,
> they are not living their own lives.[29]

Yet despite his radical attack on consciousness, Lawrence
does not want to relinquish completely the idea of consciousness. In the same work in which he asserts rather disparagingly that knowledge (the object of consciousness) is simply
the retracing of proven experience, he also concedes that "human consciousness . . . is . . . a necessary condition of the
progress of life itself."[30]

There is a dilemma in Lawrence's conception of conscious-

---

[27] "Individual Consciousness vs. Social Consciousness," *Phoenix*, p. 761.

[28] *Ibid.*   [29] *Ibid.*

[30] "Study of Thomas Hardy," *Phoenix*, p. 431.

ness from which he was never able to extricate himself completely. In a review of a book by Trigant Burrow, an unorthodox psychoanalyst with views similar to his, Lawrence cites with approval Burrow's diagnosis of "the neurosis of modern life."[31] The trouble, according to Burrow, arises not from sex repression, but from an inward sense of "separateness" which dominates every man. Burrow explains the origins of separateness:

> "It would appear that in his separativeness man has inadvertently fallen a victim to the developmental exigencies of his consciousness. Captivated by the phylogenetically new and unwonted spectacle of his own image, it would seem he has been irresistibly arrested before the mirror of his own likeness and that in the present self-conscious phase of his mental evolution he is still standing spellbound before it. . . ."[32]

Consciousness, in Lawrence's rendering of Burrow, is immediately "ideal."

> As soon as man became aware of himself, he made a picture of himself. Then he began to live according to the picture. Mankind at large made a picture of itself, and every man had to conform to the picture: the ideal.[33]

The source of human misery is man's picture-making and his "need" to live according to the picture. Lawrence explains:

> We spend all our time over the picture. All our education is but the elaborating of the picture. "A good little girl"— "a brave boy"—"a noble woman"—etc. It is all living from the outside to the inside. It is all the death of spontaneity. It is all, strictly, automatic.[34]

---

[31] Review of *The Social Basis of Consciousness*, by Trigant Burrow, *Phoenix*, p. 378.

[32] *Ibid.* [33] *Ibid.*, p. 379. [34] *Ibid.*, p. 380.

Lawrence's view of picture-making brings immediately to mind Freud's conception of the ego ideal. According to Freud, neurosis often results from the unconscious effort of man to satisfy an ideal picture of himself, which is, in its very nature, impossible of satisfaction.[35] The task of psychoanalysis is to help create within the patient enough psychic mobility so that his picture-making will have a real connection with his actual life. But Lawrence goes much further than Freud; by not distinguishing among various kinds of pictures or picture-making, he repudiates "image-consciousness" entirely, not merely its perverse manifestations. Indeed, he regards Freudian analysis itself as a substitution of one image for another image, equally destructive, "the fixed motive of the incest complex."[36] "While the Freudian theory of the unconscious and of the incest-motive is valuable as a *description* of our psychological condition, the moment you begin to *apply* it, and make it master of the living situation, you have begun to substitute one mechanism or unconscious illusion for another."[37] Lawrence's criticism is finally a criticism of consciousness itself. Every form of awareness is ultimately a form of self-awareness, and every form of self-awareness is finally a diminution of the self: "The true self is not aware that it is a self. A bird, as it sings, sings itself. But not according to a picture. It has no idea of itself."[38]

But the normative character of Lawrence's own thought, the fact that he writes novels, stories, poems, and essays in which he pictures for us a new kind of life, suggests at once difficulties in his doctrine. Man's changefulness, indeed his need to change if he is to be alive, makes the faculty of con-

---

[35] See Sigmund Freud, *Group Psychology and the Analysis of the Ego*, trans. James Strachey (London: Hogarth Press, 1948).

[36] Review of *The Social Basis of Consciousness*, *Phoenix*, p. 378.

[37] *Ibid.*   [38] *Ibid.*, p. 382.

sciousness necessary. Certainly Lawrence's belief in "the strangeness and rainbow-change of ever-renewed civilizations,"[39] and his own creative effort to renew civilization suggest the inadequacy of the image of the self that he presents in his review of Burrow's book and elsewhere. If it is not Lawrence's only view of the self, it does represent a characteristic bias—and on its positive side, an impoverishing bias. Negatively, of course, the view has its value, for it dramatizes sharply the vices of a kind of consciousness. But when Lawrence reduces all consciousness to a narcissistic self-regard, he is devaluing his own effort, which is to imagine a completely different kind of world in which men can live with real vitality. The bird may not sing according to a picture, but man, if he learns to sing like a bird, will be singing according to a picture. Without consciousness the act of imagination which Lawrence performs would be impossible and man would cease to be creative, would, that is, like the bird, repeat himself endlessly in the same song. Man differs from the bird in his possession of consciousness and, therefore, of history, and it is paradoxically his possession of both consciousness and history that makes possible the spontaneity and novelty that Lawrence finds everywhere in nature.

Lawrence's outbursts against consciousness are, as it were, the excess of his mistrust of the present tendency of consciousness to divide the self from the world and the "spirit" from the body. For man to regain possession of himself and a place in the cosmos, he must reverse the course of his history; his body in its divine aspect must overcome consciousness before consciousness itself can become once more an agent of life.

But man is a mutable animal. Turn into the Fish, the Pisces of man's final consciousness, and you'll start to swim

---

[39] *Fantasia of the Unconscious* (New York: Viking Press, 1960), p. 56.

again in the great life which is so frighteningly godly that you realize your previous presumption.[40]

Rilke, possessing the same kind of sensitivity that Lawrence possessed, speaks of man's double alienation from the life of the spirit and the life of the senses. "The experiences that are called 'appearances,' the so-called 'spirit world,' death, all those that are so closely akin to us, have by daily parrying been so driven out of life that the senses by which we could have grasped them are crippled—to say nothing of God."[41] Elsewhere, Rilke describes what he conceived to be the necessary "task of transformation."

> Not, however, in the Christian sense (from which I more and more passionately withdraw), but in a purely mundane, deeply mundane, blissfully mundane consciousness, to instate what is HERE seen and touched within the wider, within the widest orbit. . . . Nature, the things we move about among and use, are provisional and perishable; but so long as we are here, they are our possession and friendship. . . . Therefore, not only must all that is here not be corrupted and degraded . . . our task is to stamp this provisional, perishing earth into ourselves so deeply, so painfully and passionately, that its being may arise again, "invisibly," in us.[42]

The wholesale character of Lawrence's repudiation of consciousness in his review of Trigant Burrow's book and in other places is misleading, for it is possible to argue that Lawrence wanted an intensification rather than a diminution of consciousness, the kind of intensification that Rilke describes

---

[40] "The Proper Study," *Phoenix*, p. 723. The mutability of man distinguishes him from the animal, for as Lou Witt insists in *St. Mawr* man must become "all the animals in turn" (*The Short Novels*, II, 47), instead of one fixed automatic thing if he is to repossess within himself the wonder of creation.

[41] Rilke, *Letters to a Young Poet* (New York: W. W. Norton & Co., Inc., 1934), pp. 67–68.

[42] Rainer Maria Rilke, Appendix 4 to *Duino Elegies* (New York: W. W. Norton & Co., Inc., 1939), p. 128.

above. Lawrence's criticism of mind consciousness can be understood as a criticism of the soul-body dualism on which so much of the Western cultural tradition is based. To be sure, blood consciousness is often identified by Lawrence with unconscious being, but when one remembers the distinction that Lawrence makes between his own conception and the Freudian conception of the unconscious, Lawrence's meaning becomes less problematical.

III

When Lawrence first read Freud, he sensed the presence of an enemy, but like all great enemies, Freud proved a remarkable opportunity for Lawrence to define himself. *Psychoanalysis and the Unconscious* and *Fantasia of the Unconscious* are more than critical essays of Freud; they constitute what are perhaps the most definitive statements of Lawrence's ideas. The reason for this is not difficult to see. Freud's speculations on the unconscious, consciousness, the body, the passions, and sex are unrivaled by any other thinker in the modern period in interest and profundity. It is a rare opportunity for self-clarity for a thinker to confront a definitive treatment of his major themes by an adversary. In the work of Freud, Lawrence found this opportunity.

The main issue between Freud and Lawrence in *Psychoanalysis and the Unconscious* is the conception of the unconscious. Lawrence's caricature of the Freudian unconscious is vivid: "Nothing but a slimy serpent of sex, and heaps of excrement, and a myriad repulsive little horrors spawned between sex and excrement."[43] It is the ugliness of the Freudian conception that first strikes the poet, for whom the unconscious is the precious source of creativity. But Lawrence's

---

[43] *Psychoanalysis and the Unconscious* (New York: Viking Press, 1960), p. 5.

quarrel with Freud is not merely a matter of taste or temperament. Freudian doctrine, as Lawrence sees it, is faced
with a dilemma of its own making. The principal psychoanalytic explanations of neurosis are, according to Lawrence:
(1) that it is the inhibition of normal sex, and (2) that it is
the result of an unadmitted sex desire, namely incest craving.
If incest craving is not the result of inhibition, then to inhibit
it would be to induce neurosis according to the first explanation.[44]

For Lawrence the only way out is to regard incest craving
as a motive essentially alien to the unconscious, the source of
all spontaneous, "normal" desire. Invoking his own metaphysic (in which mind and blood, Lawrence's metaphor for
the unconscious, are divided and mutually antagonistic) Lawrence attributes incest craving to humanity's suppressed *idea*
of sex:

> It is nothing pristine and anterior to mentality. It is itself
> the mind's ulterior motive. That is, the incest-craving is prop-
> agated by the mind itself, even though unconsciously.[45]

Incest craving for Lawrence, in any form, at any age, is a
neurotic phenomenon. In fact, Lawrence believes that at the
deeper sensual centers there is "a radical sex-aversion between parent and child,"[46] but the mind concealing its motive
projects the incest desire illicitly into the unconscious. In
other words, the Freudian "*unconscious* does but represent our
conception of conscious sexual life as this exists in a state of
repression."[47] (Blake makes a similar judgment of the Christian moral scheme when he chooses Hell as the place to rear
his Palace of Wisdom. The evil of Hell is in the Christian
conception of it. By disengaging Hell from the Christian cos-

---

[44] See *ibid.*, p. 7.   [46] *Fantasia of the Unconscious*, p. 154.

[45] *Ibid.*, p. 8.   [47] *Psychoanalysis and the Unconscious*, p. 8.

mology, Blake restores to it energy and creativity.[48]) The analytic statements and judgments of psychoanalysis share the repressive character of the civilization it has analyzed. Norman O. Brown, working systematically within the psychoanalytic categories, arrives at a similar conclusion—and it is one of the major conclusions of his book *Life against Death*, which has been hailed as a revolutionary work. Brown's speculation about the "pregenital infantile organizations of the libido" was anticipated long ago by Lawrence in his essays on psychoanalysis. Brown writes:

> One of the central ambiguities in psychoanalytical theory is the question of whether the pregenital infantile organizations of the libido, including the anal organizations, are biologically determined. We have elsewhere taken the position that they are not biologically determined but are constructed by the human ego, or rather they represent that distortion of of the human body which *is* the human ego.[49]

The view that the pregenital infantile organizations of the libido are not biologically determined presupposes a faith in the possibility of a "resurrected body." Brown, like Lawrence before him, is at work at resurrecting the body— Brown calls it the Dionysian ego or reality. Unlike Lawrence's, Brown's resurrected body remains an abstraction. In the chapter on "The Child and His Mother" in *Psychoanalysis and the Unconscious*, Lawrence imagines the *vital* body of the child.

> In asserting that the seat of consciousness in a young infant is in the abdomen we do not pretend to suggest that all the other conscious-centres are utterly dormant. Once a child is born, the whole nervous and cerebral system comes awake, even the brain's memories begin to glimmer, recognition and

---

[48] See William Blake, *The Marriage of Heaven and Hell*.

[49] Brown, *Life against Death* (Middletown, Conn.: Wesleyan University Press, 1959), p. 191.

cognition soon begin to take place. But the spontaneous control and all the prime developing activity derived from the
great affective centres of the abdomen. In the solar plexus is
the great fountain and issue of infantile consciousness. There,
beneath the navel, lies the active human first-mind, the prime
unconscious. From the moment of conception, when the first
nucleus is formed, to the moment of death, when the nucleus
breaks again, the first great active centre of human consciousness lies in the solar plexus.[50]

"The human first-mind" is Lawrence's imaginative construct
of the true human ego of which the body is the perfect expression. The development of genuine consciousness (Lawrence uses consciousness in the positive sense and unconsciousness almost interchangeably) is very succinctly
described in the essay "Education of the People" in a kind
of summary of the doctrine put forth more elaborately in
the essays on psychoanalysis:

> the solar plexus of the abdomen is the first great affective
> centre, sympathetic, and the lumbar ganglion, volitional, is its
> partner. At these two great centres arise our first conscious-
> ness, our primary impulses, desires, motives. . . . Immedi-
> ately above the diaphragm, another great pair of conjugal
> affective centres, acting in immediate correspondence with
> the two lower centres. In these four great nerve-centres es-
> tablish the first field of our consciousness, the first plane of
> our vital being. . . . At these great centres, primarily, we live
> and move and have our being. Thought and ideas do not enter
> in. The motion arises spontaneous, we do not know how, and
> is emitted in dark vibrations. The vibration goes forth, seeks
> its object, returns, establishing a life-circuit. And this life cir-
> cuit, established internally between the four first poles, and
> established also externally between the primal affective
> centres in two different beings or creatures, this complex life
> circuit or system of circuits constitutes in itself our pro-

---

[50] *Psychoanalysis and the Unconscious*, p. 26.

found primal consciousness, and contains all our radical knowledge, knowledge non-ideal, non-mental, yet still knowledge, primary cognition, individual and potent.[51]

The extravagance of Lawrence's biology may keep one from taking these essays as seriously as they should be taken. However, even the extravagance is necessary to Lawrence's serious purpose, for to apply Norman O. Brown's description of his own book to the essays, Lawrence "did not hesitate to pursue new ideas to their ultimate 'mad' consequences."[52]

Lawrence has tried to conceive the unconscious as it might be constituted in a condition in which repression no longer exists. When ideal consciousness tries to take precedence in life by entering the domain of unconscious life, the condition of modern civilization, then "the myriad repulsive little horrors" of so-called unconscious life arise. The paradox of Freudian psychoanalysis, according to Lawrence, is that its trust in mental consciousness to achieve knowledge and control of the unconscious only intensifies the repression of genuine unconscious life. Instead of recovering the bodily passions, psychoanalysis tends to subdue and attenuate them. The self-impoverishing movement of the psyche from the mind to the solar plexus is only encouraged by psychoanalysis. Lawrence wants the movement reversed. "That which sublimates from the dynamic consciousness into the mental consciousness has alone any value."[53] And again: "Every extraneous idea, which has no root in the dynamic consciousness, is as dangerous as a nail driven into a young tree."[54]

---

[51] "Education of the People," *Phoenix*, p. 628.

[52] Brown, *Life against Death*, p. xii.

[53] *Fantasia of the Unconscious*, pp. 112–13.

[54] *Ibid.*, p. 113.

Ideal or mental consciousness is in Lawrence's conception of it the source of the self's awareness of others from which the emotions of sympathy and love develop. "It is, as it were, the adding of another self to the own self, through the mode of apprehension."[55] This capacity can be extended to infinity and become a mystical identification of the self with the whole of the universe. "A man may in his time add on to himself the whole of the universe, by increasing pristine realization of the universal."[56] The stress that Western civilization has put on this mode of consciousness, the mode of sympathy and selflessness, has had pernicious results, for the stress breaks the integrity of the soul, "and corruption sets in the living organism."[57] The pristine unconscious, freed of any determinations by mental consciousness, has as its deepest impulse "vital self-realization,"[58] the impulse to make a full bodily recoil from others and in doing so achieve independent, uncoerced selfhood. Lawrence conceives of perfect individuality as a harmony between the two modes of consciousness: "there must be the twofold passional circuit of separatist realization, the lower vital *self-realization*, and the upper, intense realization of the other, a realization which includes a recognition of abysmal *otherness*."[59]

The preservation of the harmony depends on the vigilance with which the will performs its function of maintaining the balance. "It seems as if the will were given as a great balancing faculty, the faculty whereby automatization is *prevented* in the evolving psyche."[60] Though Lawrence is generally very suspicious of the will in its tendency to become an "accomplice" of the "machine motions" and automatizations of

---

[55] *Psychoanalysis and the Unconscious*, p. 40.
[56] *Ibid.*
[57] *Ibid.*
[58] *Ibid.*, p. 41.
[59] *Ibid.*
[60] *Ibid.*, p. 47.

mind-consciousness, he regards the will in its pristine nature as "the faculty for self-determination."[61] The will is not, however, to be confused with the vitalities that Lawrence is always celebrating; it is simply the faculty "for exerting a certain control over the vital and automatic processes of [man's] own evolution."[62] That Lawrence does value the will may come as something of a surprise to a reader accustomed to his portraits of people, e.g., Hermione in *Women in Love*, whose lives are dominated by will and idea. The expression of faith in the will that concludes *Psychoanalysis and the Unconscious*, however, does not mean to raise it to a position of supremacy in Lawrence's hierarchy of values. The will, for Lawrence, remains a means, the faculty which obeys the imperative demand for change, for new harmonies.

Despite Lawrence's expression of the need for harmony between the two modes of consciousness, it is difficult not to infer from his discussion in *Psychoanalysis and the Unconscious* and elsewhere that Lawrence means to grant precedence to the dark passional (bodily) consciousness. The subordinate and passive role that mind plays in Lawrence's scheme is given in a splendid image at the end of *Apocalypse*: "There is nothing of me that is alone and absolute except my mind, and we shall find that the mind has no existence by itself, it is only the glitter of the sun on the surface of the waters."[63] In order to restore the mind to an organic unity with the bodily self, Lawrence deprives it of initiative.

The consequence of Lawrence's repudiation of mind and intellect is, however, neither diabolism nor demonic mysticism, because, in reconceiving the unconscious, Lawrence has managed to preserve many of the values of Apollonian culture. In *Fantasia of the Unconscious* Lawrence elaborated

---

[61] *Ibid.*   [62] *Ibid.*   [63] *Apocalypse*, p. 200.

his conception of a life governed by passional consciousness. Resuming his quarrel with Freud, Lawrence rejects the idea that the sexual impulse is the deepest impulse in man and consequently the essential "motivity" of the unconscious. The impulse of "higher importance, and greater dynamic power" is "the desire of the human male to build a world . . . to build up out of his own self and his own belief and his own effort something wonderful."[64] Lawrence asserts that the "religious or creative motive" is "the first motive for all human activity."[65] The unconscious is the divine presence in man from which all genuine civilization draws its energy.

In Freud, Eros, "builder of cities,"[66] is a sublimation of the sexual impulse that desires immediate gratification. The human effort to make civilization involves a relinquishing of the impulse toward immediate self-gratification—or rather its attenuation or postponement. A tension then exists within every individual and every culture between the direct expression of the sexual instinct and the need to convert it to the uses of civilized life. Though Lawrence concedes that there is "a great conflict between the interests of the two [motives, the sexual and the cultural], at all times,"[67] he inverts the metaphysical relationship between them: "the essentially religious or creative motive is the first motive for all human activity. The sexual motive comes second."[68] There is some inconsistency in Lawrence's conception of the relationship between the motives, for almost immediately after he gives primacy to the religious or creative motive, he

---

[64] *Fantasia of the Unconscious*, p. 60.

[65] *Ibid.*

[66] W. H. Auden, "In Memory of Sigmund Freud," in *The Collected Poetry of W. H. Auden* (New York: Random House, 1945), p. 167.

[67] *Fantasia of the Unconscious*, p. 60.

[68] *Ibid.*

speaks of the impulses as "man and wife, or father and son. It is no use putting one under the feet of the other."[69]

Moreover, though he concedes that a conflict between the two impulses goes on all the time, he attacks the modern desire to "assert the absolute alienity [of the religious impulse] from the sexual impulse."[70] But notwithstanding the inconsistencies, Lawrence's essential claim is clear. Civilization and culture, which have always been conceived to exist under the aegis of Apollo, the god that brings order to the wild Dionysian energies at large in the world, are conceived by Lawrence as products of those energies themselves. Lawrence conceives of culture in its ideal form as a fulfilment of the passional-visionary self, whereas Freud has the view that there exists a generic tragic opposition between the self and culture.[71]

> Even the Panama Canal would never have been built *simply* to let ships through. It is the pure disinterested craving of the human male to make something wonderful out of his own head and his own self, and his own soul's faith and delight, which starts everything going.[72]

However, "the pure disinterested craving of the human male to make something wonderful" depends on the existence of genuine individuality: "the incalculable and intangible Holy Ghost."[73] And *Fantasia of the Unconscious* is written out of the recognition that "most men are half-born slaves: the little soul they are born with just atrophies."[74] The reason for this is not to be found, and here Lawrence differs radically from Freud, in the natural evolution of mankind and human

---

[69] *Ibid.*   [70] *Ibid.*

[71] See Sigmund Freud, *Civilization and Its Discontents*, trans. Joan Riviere (New York: Jonathan Cape & Harrison Smith, 1930).

[72] *Fantasia of the Unconscious*, p. 60.

[73] *Ibid.*, p. 71.   [74] *Ibid.*

society, but in the perversion of mankind. The subject of the book is the growth of a man from infancy to adult *individual* being in which it becomes possible for a man to enter "the daylight world of men" in order to perform heroic and creative actions. Lawrence's depiction of the growth into individual being provides us with a new vision of the poverty of human life in the present world.

According to Lawrence, the destruction of the individual is the consequence of the hypertrophy of the love mode. The dynamic connection between parent and child, originating from what Lawrence calls the lower planes of consciousness, is perpetually denied by the upper sympathetic planes. "Where there is too much sympathy, then the great voluntary centres of the spine are weak, the child tends to be delicate."[75] The spine is the center of resistance and recoil, and unless it is strengthened in the son's relationship with parental authority, the son will probably be unmanned. Though Lawrence speaks of the need for a balance between the sympathetic mode and the resistant mode, the stress falls on the resistant mode. Lawrence's mistrust of "the idealism of love, of pure sympathetic communion and 'understanding,' "[76] is compatible with the findings of psychoanalysis. His account of the emasculation of the son whose relationship with his parents is defined by "love, gentleness, pity, charity" in the "serious hour of puberty"[77] is quite close to the psychoanalytic conception of the Oedipus complex.

But Lawrence's mistrust of the love mode is much deeper than Freud's. Indeed, the passional consciousness in *Fantasia of the Unconscious* is generally conceived as a bodily recoil from any connection which might confuse the self with another. And so Lawrence brings to his conception of

---

[75] *Ibid.*, p. 87.   [76] *Ibid.*, p. 150.   [77] *Ibid.*

the husband-and-wife relationship the same mistrust that he feels for the parent-child relationship. The book concludes, significantly, with an attack on what Lawrence regards as the *telos* of Freud's moral philosophy, namely, that the goal of life is sexual fulfilment. The goal of a man's life, as Lawrence conceives it, is *aloneness*:

> You've got to take a new resolution into your soul, and break off from the old way. You've got to know that you're a man, and being a man means you must go on alone, ahead of the woman, to break away through the old world, into the new. And you've got to be alone.[78]

"The theme of almost all modern tragedy,"[79]—Lawrence gives Carmen and Anna Karenina as examples—is making sex both the starting point and goal of life. Though sex, "the blood passion," is the basis of dynamic consciousness and being, the goal of a man's life must take him beyond the passional connection between man and woman. Beyond the woman, there is the world of men, and beyond that, aloneness on the frontier of the unknown.

Despite the strong female component in Lawrence's personality (which enabled him to create female characters with such remarkable sympathy), the world that Lawrence conceives is essentially a world made by and for men. The woman is defined almost completely in her relationship with the man. She believes in him, "in the pioneer which he is," and her life is "a loneliness of waiting and following."[80] Her great expectation is the return of her man from the frontier and the delight of having "again between her arms, all that she has missed, to have it poured out for her, and a richness and a wonder she had never expected."[81] The woman who re-

---

[78] *Ibid.*, p. 218.
[79] *Ibid.*, p. 219.
[80] *Ibid.*
[81] *Ibid.*, p. 220.

gards her man simply as a lover makes of their lives continual "ecstasies and agonies of love, and final passion of death."[82]

There is in *Fantasia of the Unconscious* a curious mixture of sound normative judgment and personal idiosyncrasy. It is, for instance, difficult to deny the force of Lawrence's criticism of the emasculation of modern culture. The emancipation of the woman, which has extended her power from the household to what was the world of man, has made her more and more "the responsible party, the law-giver, the culture-bearer."[83] Lawrence's sensitivity to the way in which the mother tends to victimize her son and unman him is particularly acute and discerning, and his sense of what would constitute a normal relationship between mother and son is equally unexceptionable.

> A relation between mother and child today is practically *never* parental—which means, it is critical and deliberate, and adult in provocation. The mother, in her new role of idealist and life-manager never, practically for a single moment, gives her child the unthinking response from the deep dynamic centres. . . . The poor little object is his mother's ideal. But of her head she dictates his providential days, and by the force of her deliberate mentally-directed love-will she pushes him up into boyhood. Never, never one mouthful does he drink of the mild milk of human kindness: always the sterilized milk of human benevolence. There is no mother's milk today, save in tigers' udders, and in the udders of sea-whales. Our children drink a decoction of ideal love, at the breast.[84]

But there is scarcely a "normative" judgment that is not marked by Lawrence's idiosyncratic personality. The reversal of roles between man and woman in the modern world becomes in Lawrence's paranoid version of it a ferocious battle between the sexes in which the male fights desperately for

---

[82] *Ibid.*, p. 219.   [84] *Ibid.*, p. 173.

[83] *Ibid.*, p. 172.

his dear life. The female, except in Lawrence's ideal remaking of her, is regarded as predatory.

> And so men, drive your wives, beat them out of their self-consciousness and their soft smarminess and good, lovely idea of themselves. Absolutely tear their lovely opinion of themselves to tatters. . . .
>
> But fight for your life, men. Fight your wife out of her self-conscious preoccupation with herself. Batter her out of it till she's stunned. . . . Rip all her nice superimposed modern-woman and wonderful-creature garb off her. Reduce her once more to a naked Eve, and send the apple flying.[85]

The ideal relationship that Lawrence proposes, in which man has a life *with* and *beyond* the woman, has a curious resemblance to Victorian notions of domestic bliss. The wife in Lawrence's view of her in *Fantasia* is reduced to a bed companion and a domestic.

Lawrence's belief in the primacy of the religious-creative impulse, his repudiation of the hypertrophy of the love mode (in all its forms, from Christian idealism to the sexual act itself), his insistence that the *goal* of life is in the daylight world of men in which *creative* purposes are accomplished and that even beyond that a man must be a pioneer and go out to the frontier where he can be *alone* with himself and the universe—this is what is involved in Lawrence's conception of transcendence. The implications of this view of transcendence can be seen more clearly after another look at *The Rainbow* and *Women in Love*, the novels that have the closest affinity with the essays on psychoanalysis.

IV

The Rainbow is Lawrence's most ambitious attempt to render "the night-time world" of passionate embrace between man and woman. If the nighttime world is merely the source of

---

[85] *Ibid.*, pp. 217–18.

passional life, not the goal, Lawrence nevertheless conceives it as a transcendent experience. Biblical imagery and idea are so pervasive in the novel as to constitute the atmosphere in which the characters have their life. Lawrence's description of "the great novel" applies equally to the Bible and *The Rainbow*.

> In every great novel, who is the hero all the time? Not any of the characters, but some unnamed and nameless flame behind them all. . . . In the great novel the felt but unknown flame stands behind all the characters, and in their words and gestures there is a flicker of the presence.[86]

Lawrence's technique for rendering the presence of the great nameless flame behind his characters is similar to the biblical technique as described in *Mimesis* by Eric Auerbach.

Like the Bible, *The Rainbow* is, in Eric Auerbach's words, "fraught with background."[87] Like Abraham, the Laurentian characters, i.e., those capable of fulfilment, direct their actions "toward the depths of the picture or upward."[88] The fulfilment of Tom and Lydia after two years of married life is achieved as suddenly as the appearance of God in the Abraham story: it is the sudden unwilled revelation of divinity in their souls. If Lydia had failed to fulfil herself in Paul Lensky, it was because "God had passed through the married pair without fully making Himself known to them."[89]

> Now He was declared to Brangwen and to Lydia Brangwen, as they stood together. When at last they had joined hands, the house was finished, and the Lord took up his abode. And they were glad.

---

[86] *The Later D. H. Lawrence*, p. 193.

[87] Eric Auerbach, *Mimesis*, trans. Willard Trask (New York: Doubleday Anchor Books, 1957), p. 9.

[88] *Ibid.*, p. 7.

[89] *The Rainbow* (London: William Heinemann, Ltd., 1957), p. 92.

The days went on as before, Brangwen went out to his work, his wife nursed her child and attended in some measure to the farm. They did not think of each other—why should they? Only when she touched him, he knew her instantly, and she was with him, near him, that she was the gateway and the way out, that she was beyond, and that he was travelling in her through the beyond. Whither?—What does it matter? He responded always. When she called, he answered, when he asked, her response came at once, or at length.[90]

As in the Abraham story, the social and material texture of the narrative is a translucent medium through which divinity reveals itself. Brangwen's work and Lydia's nursing are presented with the economy one finds in a biblical narrative—without an epithet or qualifying clause. They are there to serve Lawrence's primary purpose to render the *beyond*.

Auerbach's description of Abraham's journey ("the journey is like a silent progress through the indeterminate and the contingent"[91]) applies to *The Rainbow*. Neither space nor time is permitted to inhibit action in the beyond. For instance, there is the description of the first fulfilment of Tom and Lydia:

He felt the tension breaking up in him, his fists slackened, he was unable to move. He stood there looking at her, helpless in his vague collapse. For the moment she had become unreal to him, curiously direct and as if without movement, in a sudden flow. She put her hand to his coat.

He turned and looked for a chair, and keeping her still in his arms, he sat down with her close to him, to his breast. Then for a few seconds, he went utterly to sleep, asleep and sealed in the darkest sleep, utter, extreme oblivion.

From which he came to gradually, always holding her warm and close upon him, and she as utterly silent as he, involved in the same oblivion, the fecund darkness.

---

[90] *Ibid.*   [91] Auerbach, *Mimesis*, p. 7.

He returned gradually, but newly created, as after a gestation, a new birth, in the womb of darkness. Aerial and light everything was, new as a morning, fresh and newly begun. And she sat utterly still with him, as if the same.[92]

The movement in this passage cannot be measured in time and space. Lydia "comes to him direct and as if *without movement*, in a *sudden flow*." The oxymoronic effect is deliberate. We are in a fluid world in which movement can occur suddenly, in an instant. The withdrawing and emerging are immediate; they leave no traces, for the movement is immanent in the souls of the characters. The social world, the world of space and time, is shut out. In the new world into which they have entered, which is at once beyond and within them, Lydia and Tom have become fulfilled, complete unto themselves.

She was oddly concerned, even as if it pleased her a little. He sat and listened and wondered. It was rather splendid, to be so ignored by her, whilst she lay against him, and he lifted her with his breathing, and felt her weight upon his living, so he had a completeness and an inviolable power. He did not even know her. He did not interfere with her. It was so strange that she lay there with her weight abandoned upon him. He was silent with delight. He felt strong, physically, carrying her on his breathing. The strange, inviolable completeness of the two of them made him feel as sure and as stable as God. . . .[93]

And yet despite the transcendent nature of the passional connections between the men and women, there is throughout the novel a pervasive sense of their inadequacy. Even at the moment of transcendence the qualifying note is struck. ("When she called, he answered, when he asked, her response came at once, or at length.")[94] One is first tempted to explain

---

[92] *The Rainbow*, pp. 40–41.   [93] *Ibid.*, p. 42.   [94] *Ibid.*, p. 92.

this on the basis of what seems to be Lawrence's vision of the ritual movement of life itself. Every fulfilment is momentary: the moment that precedes new dissatisfactions, new imbalances, new life. The rhythm of *The Rainbow*, and to a lesser extent this is true of the other novels, corresponds to the cycle of fulfilment, dissatisfaction, fulfilment, etc. This is why, one might argue, none of the novels is "resolved." Every resolution precedes another dissatisfaction, another urge to make forays into the unknown. The difficulty with this explanation, however, is that it ignores the discriminations that are made between the Brangwen men and the Brangwen women and the discriminations made between the Brangwen men themselves. The failure of each relationship is particular, arising from failures in the characters themselves.

The opening pages distinguish the Brangwen men, who face "inwards to the teeming life of creation,"[95] from the women, who wanting "another form of life than this, something that was not blood intimacy," face "outwards to where men moved dominant and creative, having turned their back on the pulsing heat of creation, and with this behind them, set out to discover what was beyond, to enlarge their own scope and range and freedom."[96] The "form of life" that the women desire is the religious life proposed in *Fantasia of the Unconscious*. By attributing this desire to the women, Lawrence is making his case for this form of life in the most conclusive manner possible, for it is the female, "naked Eve"— the woman in her pristine, unspoiled aspect—that is most capable of recognizing the true male. Thus Tom Brangwen, whose whole life was absorbed first by his wife Lydia and then by his daughter Anna, is drowned in the flood. The symbolic implication of the drowning is unmistakable, for it oc-

---

[95] *Ibid.*, p. 3.   [96] *Ibid.*

curs when Tom is almost hypnotically drawn to the source
of the raging river. The drowning is the punishment appropriate to one who has "faced inwards to the teeming life of
creation." The failure of Will's relationship with Anna, on
the other hand, stems from his *wilful* rejection of the night-
time life with Anna, his attempt on occasion to impose his
will on her and his passion for spiritual transcendence cli-
maxed by his mystical experience on his visit to Lincoln
Cathedral.

In the light of the transcendent nature of the consummations between the men and women, the novel's sense of the
inadequacy of the loves is somewhat puzzling. Lawrence's formula for the passional life remains a formula, unless it is made
to correspond with the reader's immediate sense of the inadequacy of the loves, unless, that is, we are given a glimpse
of the "far-off world of cities and governments and the active
scope of man,"[97] which both Tom and Will each in his own
way deny, or the experience of aloneness with the cosmos
that is necessary, in Lawrence's view, to true male being and
without which the act of love is an emasculation.

In Birkin, the protagonist of *Women in Love*, the crisis of
the Laurentian male achieves its greatest clarity, and in Birkin's relationship to Ursula, to Gerald, and to the social
"world" of the novel, we can see more accurately than elsewhere in Lawrence the meaning or goal of Laurentian transcendence.

As many critics have pointed out, the relationship between
Birkin and Ursula is intended to represent the expansion and
realization of vitalities in them, while the relationship between Gudrun and Gerald develops, in contrast, toward ca-
tastrophe and death. The love of Birkin and Ursula, however,
is successful only by contrast with the disastrous connection

---

[97] *Ibid.*

between Gerald and Gudrun, for if we ignore the counter-pointing of the two relationships and consider simply the evolution of Birkin in the novel, then the "fulfilment" of his relationship with Ursula seems a rather dubious affair. What characterizes Birkin's action throughout the novel is a search for transcendent states of being, and that search draws him away from women, not toward them. Thus Birkin's desire to break free from Hermione cannot be explained exclusively as a recoil from the predatory female. To be sure, Hermione in her awful wilfulness is an enemy of life and spontaneity, and Birkin's flight from her is the necessary act of self-preservation. But Birkin's suspicion of Hermione reflects a deeper suspicion of "the eternal feminine." The recoil from Hermione remains a constant posture in Birkin which determines his relations with Ursula. Again Birkin's violent and suspicious behavior toward Ursula cannot be explained as the suspiciousness of a man who has been burned badly by a particularly noxious female. His recoil from Ursula is a recoil from "the eternal feminine" in her, and it is graphically illustrated by the episode in which Birkin tries to destroy the reflection of the moon upon the water. The image, of course, is indestructible, and Birkin's anger finally releases his passion for Ursula. The "mystic" consummation in darkness, however, is short-lived, and the battle goes on between them.

If we consider the consummation itself, or the "love ethic" that Lawrence attaches to it, we can perhaps begin to appreciate the extent of Birkin's recoil from the act of love. The merging of identities, what the Elizabethans called "the little death," is passionately repudiated by Birkin. Instead the act of love becomes a male-female polarity, or in one of Lawrence's metaphors "a star equilibrium,"[98] in which the sepa-

---

[98] See *Women in Love* (London: William Heinemann, Ltd., 1957), chapter xix.

rate identities of the lovers are maintained even at the moment of consummation. Even Ursula, who insists at the end of the novel that Birkin is her whole life, rejects love as an ideal. Ursula makes the rejection in an argument with Gudrun toward the end of the novel.

> ". . . Love is too human and little. I believe in something inhuman of which love is only a part. I believe that what we must fulfill comes out of the unknown to us, and it is something infinitely more than love. It isn't so merely human."[99]

Given Ursula's statement at the end of the novel that Birkin is enough for her, "I don't want anybody else but you,"[100] Ursula's little speech to Gudrun seems like a justification of Birkin's life, not her own life. It is as if Lawrence wanted a confirming statement from Ursula to vindicate Birkin's actions to the reader.

The suspicious critic, oriented to psychoanalysis, sees in this rejection of love and of woman a concealment of "a fear [in Birkin], perhaps as deep as, or deeper than, his longing for Ursula."[101] The critic has only to invoke in support of this view Birkin's strange relationship with Gerald, particularly as it is expressed in the homoerotic wrestling episode and the peculiar note of discontent on which the novel ends in which Birkin expresses his desire for "eternal union with a man."[102] Birkin, from this point of view, suffers from a homosexual fear of women.[103]

That there is something in this view can be denied only by one whose commitment to the Laurentian ethos is fanatical.

---

[99] *Ibid.*, p. 429.   [100] *Ibid.*, p. 472.

[101] Vivas, *D. H. Lawrence: The Failure and the Triumph of Art* (Evanston: Northwestern University Press, 1960), p. 260.

[102] *Women in Love*, p. 473.

[103] His critical tact, perhaps a trifle overscrupulous, prevents Vivas from stating this outright, but his implication is unmistakable. See Vivas, *D. H. Lawrence: The Failure and Triumph of Art*, pp. 255–72.

But the homosexual impulse in Birkin is extremely inadequate to explain the *experience* that is gained by a rejection of a love all "too human and little"—that experience of the "unknown" of which the passionate embraces of Birkin and Ursula do give us a glimpse and of which there is an intimation in Birkin's speculations, occasioned by his viewing of an elegant sculptured figure from West Africa, in which he speaks of the African "process" as a "further sensual experience—something deeper, darker, than ordinary life can give."[104] Birkin earlier described the African way as "pure culture in sensation, culture in the physical consciousness, mindless, utterly sensual."[105] Birkin rejects the African way because it involves dreadful mysteries beyond the phallic cult. He asks himself, "How far in their inverted culture, had these West Africans gone beyond phallic knowledge?"[106] And in imagining the distance—"the goodness, the holiness, the desire for creation must have lapsed"[107]—Birkin recoils in fear from it.

The mysteries from which he recoils are doubtless Dionysian mysteries, the marvelous and terrible experience in which man is "led back to the very heart of nature." Birkin wants the experience of oneness with the cosmic energy, and for this reason the love of a woman, though it may lead to contact with that energy, is finally limiting ("too human and little"). Much as he wants that experience, however, he does not want to be devoured by it. What he desires, and it is implicit in every description of Birkin at the moment of sexual consummation (e.g., "he felt as if he were seated in immemorial potency"),[108] is to be, as it were, the point at

---

[104] *Women in Love*, p. 245.

[105] *Ibid.*, p. 72.

[106] *Ibid.*, p. 246.

[107] *Ibid.*, p. 245.

[108] *Ibid.*, p. 310.

which all the energies of the universe converge and where he can experience them incarnate in his being as sheer *power*—in a word, Dionysian oneness between man and the cosmos becomes the complete fulfilment of the self.

The experience of oneness with the cosmos not only transcends personality in the ordinary sense: it transcends sex itself. The self becomes a hermaphroditic unity engaged in a kind of sexual intercourse with itself. In his remarkable book *Christ and Nietzsche*, G. Wilson Knight characterizes the "hermaphroditic state [as] pre-eminently the creative state."[109] What is involved is passive (feminine) receptivity to the inspirational flow into consciousness and an active (masculine) exertion of the will to re-create the world. The analogues to Laurentian transcendence are Zarathustra's colloquies with his own soul, Yeats's with his "anti-self" and Whitman's encounters and mergings on the open road.[110] The leap beyond oneself is the leap into a greater possession of one's powers. The living connection with the universe occurs within the egocentric circle of the self.

The doctrine of "disquality" that Birkin enunciates, in which he asserts the essential incomparableness of all human beings,[111] comes out of Lawrence's belief in transcendence as a way which liberates the self from the diminutions of social life and leads to oneness with the cosmic order. There is always, to be sure, the danger of disintegration or annihilation.[112]

---

109 G. Wilson Knight, *Christ and Nietzsche: An Essay in Poetic Wisdom* (London: Staples Press, 1948), p. 151.

110 See *ibid.*, p. 180. This will be qualified in the next chapter in the discussion of Lawrence's view of Whitman.

111 "Spiritually, there is pure difference and neither equality nor inequality counts. . . . I, myself, who am myself, what have I to do with equality with any other man or woman?" (*Women in Love*, p. 96).

112 The experience of annihilation and disintegration "beyond phallic knowledge" is explored in "The Woman Who Rode Away," which is discussed in the next chapter.

The right connection with the cosmos is the abiding preoccupation of Lawrence's work, and in the novels and tales that followed *Women in Love*, Lawrence, abandoning what he called the love mode, sought a new life mode through which man might achieve the potency of complete selfhood in organic connection with "the living incarnate cosmos."[113]

---

[113] *Apocalypse*, p. 200.

5

The Reciprocity of Power

The "middle period," in which he wrote *Aaron's Rod, Kangaroo*, and *The Plumed Serpent*,[1] has been largely regarded as a time of artistic failure for Lawrence. One critic typically speaks of the breakdown of Lawrence's "aesthetic of emotional form [which] . . . coincides with the troubled middle period of his life—the period stretching from *The Lost Girl* through *Aaron's Rod, Kangaroo, The Boy in the Bush* and *The Plumed Serpent*." The exclusion of these novels from Lawrence's major canon is unfortunate, for despite their serious faults, they embody significant characteristics of Lawrence's achievement and help us immeasurably in understanding his earlier and later work. The biographical explanation that the war and the legalizing of his marriage to Frieda created, as it were, a dislocation in Lawrence's imagination suggests mistakenly that the novels are temporary aberrations.[2] The embittered, repudiating, misanthropic mood of *Aaron's Rod* and *Kangaroo* is no accident of circumstance. The mood of repudiation is already very strong in *Women in Love*—as it is in *St. Mawr* and *The Captain's Doll*, tales of "the troubled middle period," the artistic successes of which, strangely

---

[1] Mark Spilka, *The Love Ethic of D. H. Lawrence* (Bloomington: Indiana University Press, 1957), p. 31.

[2] See Diana Trilling (ed.), Introduction to *The Selected Letters of D. H. Lawrence* (New York: Farrar, Straus & Cudahy, 1958), p. xxv.

enough, have never been challenged by the critics who connect the failures of *Aaron's Rod* and *Kangaroo* with the war
and his marriage.

In *Aaron's Rod* there is a complete repudiation of "the love-
mode"—the fulfilment of a tendency already present in *Women
in Love*. But the repudiation is so complete that we experience
the novels as worlds apart. After all, despite the dissatisfactions in the passional connection between Birkin and Ursula, the novel is about their passion. *Women in Love* is a love
novel, which neither *Aaron's Rod* nor *Kangaroo* is. The polarity idea, "the love-ethic" of *Women in Love*, is affirmed as a
possibility in *Aaron's Rod*, but it is never given dramatic actuality. Aaron's encounter with the Marchesa, the one significant erotic episode in the novel,[3] only confirms Aaron's decision to fight the love ideal. Love has died for Lawrence, at
least for the time being.

As I have tried to show in the preceding chapter, Lawrence
in a sense was never a love poet. Love as the recognition of
the limitations of the self, of the presence of deity in the *other*
and of the consequent need to submit to the other, was never
very congenial to Lawrence. His preference is for the personal body, which has arrogated to itself divinity.[4] Though
he speaks in his "Study of Hardy" of the necessary harmony of love and law, Lawrence means to give us "senses,

---

[3] See *Aaron's Rod* (London: William Heinemann, Ltd., 1954), chapter xviii.

[4] Though Lawrence speaks here and elsewhere of the need to submit to the
gods in the other persons as well as to the god in one's own body, both his life
and his work show an obsession with the god in his own body. Lawrence's
friends were for the most part second-rate people who existed for Lawrence
as disciples. A friend of the stature of Joyce or Yeats would have been, I think,
unimaginable. It is also interesting that when Lawrence read the works of men
of genius at least equal to and probably greater than his own and whose gods
were different, he was incapable of making a sensitive response. "Water Jelly,"
he says of Proust, and *The Charterhouse of Parma* elicited the impertinence
"emotionally trashy" (*The Letters of D. H. Lawrence* [London: William Heinemann, Ltd., 1956], pp. 21, 716).

sensation, sensuousness, these things which are incontrovert-ibly Me," the law, the way of the body. The presence of the other in the earlier work means for Lawrence no surrender of the self to the other. On the contrary, at the moment of con-summation there is a kind of "erotic solipsism"[5] in which the man secured in his maleness and the woman in her femaleness are separate though connected. This occurs under ideal con-ditions, that is, when the woman submits to the man, demand-ing neither love nor devotion.

In *The Rainbow* and *Women in Love* the erotic solipsism was still possible. There is relatively little danger to the self, the bodily self, from the presence of the *other*. In the novels that follow, so strongly is the presence of the *other* felt as coercive that the heroes live, so to speak, in an atmosphere of "sheer repudiation." Aaron's creed is unequivocal:

> As for future unisons, too soon to think about it. Let there
> be clean and pure division first, perfected singleness. That is
> the only way to final, living unison: through sheer, finished
> singleness.[6]

To be sure, Aaron (or rather Lawrence speaking for Aaron) looks forward to "future unisons," but his goal in the novel is "perfected singleness." The nighttime and daytime worlds, as they are conceived in the psychoanalytic essays, *The Rain-bow*, and *Woman in Love*, do not apply to *Aaron's Rod* or *Kangaroo*. The renewal of life no longer has its source in the passionate encounter between men and women, the meta-physic of Lawrence's earlier period. Love at the contempo-rary moment had become a bullying action of the will, an exertion rather than a spontaneous motion of the soul.

---

[5] See Eliseo Vivas, *D. H. Lawrence: The Failure and the Triumph of Art* (Evanston: Northwestern University Press, 1960), pp. 125–36. I appropriate the phrase "erotic solipsism" from Vivas and invest it with a meaning differ-ent from his.

[6] *Aaron's Rod*, p. 123.

Studies in Classic American Literature, with its keen mistrust of "the love-mode," belongs to this period in Lawrence's imaginative career. Apart from its considerable value as criticism in depth of American literature, the *Studies* must be read as part of the unfolding drama of Lawrence's imagination. Lawrence, it must be remembered, was neither casual nor professional in his criticism. He made his criticism out of the same heat that he made his novels, tales, and poems, and he wrote only about writers with whom he felt a real connection, either through sympathy or aversion. The discoveries he makes in his readings of the classic American authors are comparable to those made in his novels and tales. The American writers become part of the fabric of his own imagination.

In the essay on Poe, Lawrence speaks of American "art activity" as being dual: "1. A disintegrating and sloughing off of the old consciousness. 2. A forming of a new consciousness underneath."[7] The rhythm of American literature is the rhythm of Lawrence's own art, which is concerned with the sloughing-off of an old and dying consciousness and the forming of a new consciousness. The old and dying consciousness is the love urge in its path to death.

> Love is the mysterious vital attraction which draws things together, closer, closer together. For this reason sex is the actual crisis of love. For in sex the two blood systems, in the male and female, concentrate and come into contact, the merest film intervening. Yet if the intervening film breaks down, it is death.[8]

Wherever love is presented in American literature, Lawrence, with his peculiar sensitivity to its exhaustion in the modern European psyche, discovers diabolism and destruction. Despite the chanting "Love and produce! Love and pro-

---

[7] *Studies in Classic American Literature* (New York: Doubleday Anchor Books, 1953), p. 73.

[8] *Ibid.*, p. 74.

duce!"[9] that comes from the upper consciousness, the whole passion of the under-consciousness is directed toward destruction and death.

The new consciousness that is forming underneath the old dying consciousness is prefigured in terms of friendship rather than love. Lawrence finds the beginnings of the new consciousness in the friendship of Fenimore Cooper's Chingachook and Natty Bumppo.

> What did Cooper dream beyond democracy? Why, in his immortal friendship of Chingachook and Natty Bumppo he dreamed the nucleus of a new society. That is, he dreamed a new relationship. A stark, stripped human relationship of two men, deeper than the deeps of sex. Deeper than property, deeper than fatherhood, deeper than marriage, deeper than love. So deep that it is loveless. The stark, loveless, wordless unison of two men who have come to the bottom of themselves. This is the new nucleus of a new society, the clue to a new epoch. It asks for a great and cruel sloughing first of all. Then it finds a great release into a new world, a new moral, a new landscape.[10]

The nature of "the unison of two men" remains something of an abstraction in the book, though Lawrence is careful to distinguish it from the love bond. Indeed, his criticism of Whitman is based on the sense that the love bond and the "sympathetic" bond are present in confusion in Whitman. Thus instead of asserting the need for a connection with others that would respect the separate identities of the persons in the relationship, Whitman wanted to embrace and merge with others. "This merging *en masse*, One Identity, Myself monomania was a carry-over from the old Love idea."[11] The passion for merging in love, for the obliteration of identity and distinction, Lawrence understands as a demo-

---

[9] *Ibid.*, p. 93.   [10] *Ibid.*, p. 63.   [11] *Ibid.*, p. 186.

cratic passion, as the passion for death. But there is a true democracy in which souls on the open road encounter each other and make connection without dissolving their individual identities. According to Lawrence, Whitman is at his best the prophet of this true democracy of which Cooper also had dreamed.

Lawrence's criticism of the Whitmanian ALL can be reconciled with the longing of the Laurentian hero for oneness with the cosmos, if we remember that the cosmos is at once an opportunity and a danger to the self. The cosmos can either enhance or overwhelm the self, and when Lawrence, in a famous passage, censures Whitman for identifying himself with the Negro slave and prostitute—"a sinking of Walt Whitman's soul in the souls of these others"[12]—he is speaking out of his own dread of the diminution of the self through merging.

Vague as Lawrence is about the new consciousness which he believed was forming in America, his vision of the destruction of the old consciousness is very vivid. "The Woman Who Rode Away," in a sense Lawrence's own contribution to classic American literature, is the *ne plus ultra* of his imagination of the destruction of the white psyche in America. The unnamed heroine of the tale, married to a man not "exactly magical to her,"[13] discovers at the age of thirty-three that "her conscious development had stopped mysteriously with her marriage."[14] Her husband is one of Lawrence's industrial tycoons, all energy on the outside but dead within. Bored and oppressed by the marriage, the woman decides to "get out" and wander beyond the "little Spanish town" and

---

[12] *Ibid.*, p. 187.
[13] "The Woman Who Rode Away," in *The Complete Short Stories* (London: William Heinemann, Ltd., 1957), II, 546.
[14] *Ibid.*, p. 547.

visit "the secret haunts of these timeless, mysterious, marvellous Indians of the mountains."[15]

Her encounter with the Indians is one of the strangest of the many strange things that occur in Lawrence. Even before her meeting with the Indians, she feels on "the silent, fatal-seeming mountain slopes . . . like a woman who has died and passed beyond."[16] This is a prefiguration of the actual death that she will experience at the hands of the Indians, who will offer her up as a sacrifice to their God—a symbolic gesture signifying that the power is passing from the white race to them. What is extraordinary is the mixture of indifference and fascination with which the woman goes to her death, the supreme confidence that she seems to have in the knowledge that she is fulfilling her "destiny." The relationship between her and the Indians is defined by the look of the young Indian who first comes upon her. "His eyes were quick and black, and inhuman."[17] And again when she meets the elder men of the tribe, their glances, too, are "intense, remote, and inhuman."[18] In their eyes her personal character, her very womanliness, dissolves—"as if, perhaps, her whiteness took away all her womanhood."[19] There are moments on the long climb to the top of the mountain when even in her weariness with the "White God" she experiences a sense of outrage and bewilderment. The old self has not completely died, and the woman wonders about her persistence in crawling up the sheets of rock: "Why she did not hurl herself down, and have done!"[20] But the demonic fascination with dark men and the fierce impersonal gleam in their eyes impel her hypnotically to her "fulfilment" in death. The

---

[16] *Ibid.*, p. 548–49.   [18] *Ibid.*, p. 557.

[16] *Ibid.*, p. 551.   [19] *Ibid.*, p. 558.

[17] *Ibid.*, p. 554.   [20] *Ibid.*

divestment of her personal womanhood, which at first angers and amazes her, becomes the source of both pain and pleasure.

> Her kind of womanhood, intensely personal and individual, was to be obliterated again, and the great primeval symbols were to tower once more over the fallen individual independence of woman. The sharpness and the quivering nervous consciousness of the highly-bred white woman was to be destroyed again, womanhood was to be cast once more into the great stream of impersonal sex and impersonal passion. Strangely, as if clairvoyant, she saw the immense sacrifice prepared. And she went back to her little house in a trance of agony.[21]

And shortly afterwards, she had the "exquisite sense of bleeding out into the higher beauty and harmony of things."[22]

The state of consciousness into which the woman enters and of which the ritual fire is the supreme moment has been characterized by Nietzsche in *The Birth of Tragedy:* "all of Nature's excess in joy, sorrow, and knowledge become audible, even in piercing shrieks."[23] It is the Dionysian festival in which the women who participate in the rites are led back to "the heart of nature" and brought face to face with the naked energy of the cosmos—the sun in Lawrence's metaphor in "The Woman Who Rode Away" and elsewhere. The woman in Lawrence's terrible parable thus becomes the surrogate consciousness (for the reader) of an entry into a new kind of life—beyond society, love, or even sex. ("She was the more puzzled, as there was nothing sensual or sexual in the look. It has a terrible glittering purity that was beyond her."[24]) This experience, from which Birkin recoiled in his speculations about the inverted culture of the "African way,"

---

[21] *Ibid.*, pp. 569–70.   [22] *Ibid.*, p. 572.

[23] Nietzsche, *The Birth of Tragedy*, in *The Philosophy of Nietzsche* (New York: Modern Library, 1950), p. 967.

[24] "The Woman Who Rode Away," in *The Complete Short Stories*, III, 560.

holds the secret of power which the Laurentian hero desires
to possess.

> Only the eyes of the oldest man were not anxious. Black,
> and fixed, and as if sightless they watched the sun, seeing
> beyond the sun. And in their black, empty concentration
> there was power, power intensely abstract and remote, but
> deep, deep to the heart of the earth, and the heart of the sun.
> In absolute motionlessness he watched till the red sun should
> send his ray through the column of ice. Then the old man
> would strike, and strike home, accomplish the sacrifice and
> achieve the power.[25]

Nowhere in Lawrence is the risk of transcendence presented
with such graphic intensity as in "The Woman Who Rode
Away." The tale ends on a triumphant note—"the mastery
that man must hold, and that passes from race to race"[26]—
but the note of danger has also been struck.

The Captain's Doll presents the power urge in the context
of a love story, and the effect is bizarre and disconcerting.
The exchanges between the captain and Hannele are strangely marked by the captain's aloofness, which in the paradoxical way of the tale becomes the basis of their relationship. At
first, Hannele is bewildered and troubled by his "odd way of
answering as if he were only half-attending, as if he were
thinking of something else."[27] But it is precisely this aloofness
that compels her toward him.

> He lifted his brows and looked at her. Her heart always
> melted when he looked straight at her with his black eyes,
> and that curious, bright unseeing look that was more like
> second-sight than direct vision. She never knew what he saw
> when he looked at her.[28]

---

[25] *Ibid.*, p. 581.   [26] *Ibid.*

[27] *The Captain's Doll*, in *The Short Novels* (London: William Heinemann, Ltd., 1956), I, 7.

[28] *Ibid.*, p. 9.

And in the extraordinary ending to the tale, Hannele finally capitulates to the captain's demand for adoration and his refusal to love her. The mesmerism that the captain exerts is never given a name, but its reality is unmistakably conveyed by the episode at the hotel in which the captain pits himself against the mountains. After insisting, against "the wonder and ridicule" of Hannele, that the mountains "are less than me," he sets out to climb them in order to show his mastery over them.[29] The captain returns, properly impressed with "the wonder, the terror and the bitterness of it."[30] He "prefers the world where cabbages will grow on the soil" to the frozen mountain where there is "never a warm leaf to unfold, never a gesture of life to give off."[31] But the captain has not been humbled. He remains the "megalomaniac" that he was before the climb, and it is this "megalomania" that is the substance of what draws Hannele to him. The word "megalomaniac" is thrown out by Hannele in a fit of anger and resistance,[32] but it points, if negatively, to the new life mode that Lawrence has embraced. This new life mode is described by Lilly, the spokesman for Lawrence's ideas in *Aaron's Rod.*

> "We've exhausted the love-urge, for the moment. And yet we try to force it to continue working. So we get inevitably anarchy and murder. It's no good. We've got to accept the power motive, accept it in deep responsibility, do you understand me? It is a great life-motive. It was the great dark power-urge which kept Egypt so intensely living for so many centuries. It is a vast dark source of life and strength in us now, waiting either to issue into true action, or to burst into cataclysm. Power—the power-urge. The will-to-power—but not in Nietzsche's sense. Not intellectual power.

---

[29] *Ibid.*, p. 69.
[30] *Ibid.*, p. 75.
[31] *Ibid.*, p. 76.
[32] *Ibid.*, p. 70.

Not mental power. Not conscious will-power. Not even wisdom. But dark, fructifying power.[33]

Hannele's bafflement at the captain's behavior wins our sympathy perhaps more than Lawrence intended:

> "Is he mad? What does he mean? Is he a madman? He wants to bully me into something. What does he want to bully me into? Does he want me to love him?"[34]

Impressive as the tale is, *The Captain's Doll* reveals the temporary exhaustion of Lawrence's erotic imagination; the sensuousness of the earlier work is absent from the tale. The pitched battle between Hannele and the captain is conducted through words and gestures, through aloofness and anger; the physical connection between them is minimal. Why, one wonders, should the captain bother to marry Hannele under any circumstances? For the power urge is "self-central, not seeking its centre outside, in some God or beloved, but acting indomitably from within itself."[35]

In *Aaron's Rod* the power urge descends suddenly upon Aaron, and though it is not defined until later, when Aaron meets Lilly, Lawrence's articulate spokesman, the power urge is the immediate cause of Aaron's flight from his family. In the chapter "More Pillar of Salt" Aaron returns to his wife as suddenly, as gratuitously, as he left her, but again the urge, as yet unexpressed, works darkly within him, and he recoils once again from the connection with her.

> "What have you come for?" she cried again with a voice full of hate. Or perhaps it was fear and doubt and even hope as well. He heard only hate.
>
> This time he turned to look at her. The old dagger was drawn in her.

---

[33] *Aaron's Rod*, p. 288.

[34] *The Captain's Doll*, in *The Short Novels*, I, 70.

[35] *Aaron's Rod*, p. 288.

"I wonder," he said, "myself."

"You know you've been wrong to me, don't you?" she said, half wistfully, half menacingly.

He felt her wistfulness and menace tearing him in his bowels and loins.

"You do know, don't you?" she insisted, still with the wistful appeal, and the veiled threat.

"You do, or you would answer," she said. "You've still got enough that's right in you, for you to know."

She waited. He sat still, as if drawn by hot wires.

Then she slipped across to him, put her arms around him, sank on her knees at his side, and sank her face against his thigh.

. . . it half overcame, and at the same time, horrified him. He had a certain horror of her. The strange, liquid sound of her appeal seemed to him like the swaying of a serpent which mesmerizes the fated, fluttering, helpless bird. She clasped her arms around him, she drew him to her, she half-roused his passion. At the same time she coldly horrified and repelled him. He had not the faintest feeling at the moment of his own wrong. But she wanted to win his own self-betrayal out of him. He could see himself as the fascinated victim, falling to this cajoling, artful woman, the wife of his bosom. But as well, he had a soul outside himself, which looked on the scene with cold revulsion and which was as unchangeable as time.

"No," he said. "I don't feel wrong."[36]

I have given the scene at some length, because it has been part of the evidence for a case against *Aaron's Rod* which does not do adequate justice to Lawrence's intention. Eliseo Vivas fails to see the rightness of Lawrence's approval of Aaron's leaving his wife. The evidence for Lottie as a dominating and complaining woman is not sufficiently realized for Vivas to accept Aaron's (or Lawrence's) account of the situation.[37] Vivas, refusing to trust the artist, claims that the tale reveals

---

[36] *Ibid.*, pp. 118, 121–22.
[37] See Vivas, *D. H. Lawrence: The Failure and the Triumph of Art*, pp. 29–35.

a connection between "Aaron's reaction to Lottie, his sense of frustration with her and the children," and "the strange relationship between Lilly and Aaron."[38]

Vivas' Freudian reading of *Aaron's Rod*, as well as of *Women in Love*, simply deprives Lawrence of his *radical* vision of the generic failure of the erotic connection between man and woman. Leavis' defense of Lawrence's attitude toward Aaron, which Vivas misunderstands, is based on the right understanding of the radical criticism that Lawrence is making.

> It is a familiar situation, a familiar kind of life—frustrating deadlock. The presenting of it transcends ordinary moral judgments; to judge Aaron selfish and irresponsible for leaving his wife in the lurch with the children on her hands (though he provides for her financially), or to say that, whatever the total account of rights and wrongs might be, plainly the domineering, demanding, complaining woman was at fault and had made his life intolerable, wouldn't, we know, be to the point. The presenting sensibility and the inquiring intelligence engaged are, of course, profoundly and essentially moral; the moral concern goes far deeper than the level of those judgments. What is wrong here? What laws of life have been ignored that there should be *this* situation, this dreadful deadlock between a man and a woman? These questions give the informing preoccupation.[39]

Leavis' implicit presumption is that a man fully possessed of his manhood, untainted by a "strange relationship" with another man, might experience this sense of "frustrating deadlock" with a woman who is not "domineering, demanding, complaining." Indeed, the "strange relationship" with another man might be the outcome of what Denis de Rougemont, describing the attitude toward love in the period in

---

[38] *Ibid.*, p. 31.

[39] F. R. Leavis, *D. H. Lawrence: Novelist* (New York: Alfred A. Knopf, 1956), p. 28.

which *Aaron's Rod* was written, has characterized as the feeling that "the individual relations of the sexes had ceased to be the most appropriate theater for passion to occur in."[40] To reduce this feeling immediately to concealed or illicit motives is to disallow the possibility that the norms of a civilization might be an inadequate measure of the energies and actions of its men and women. It is, in other words, to disallow a criticism of the norms themselves. Whatever the "moral" wrongness or rightness of Aaron's actions, the fact remains that both Aaron and Lottie (the "he" and "she" in the passages quoted above) are shown to be two resistant, mortally opposed natures whose very lives depend on their opposition to one another. In Lottie's hatred for Aaron and in the "one black unconscious movement" in which Aaron leaves we have a concrete manifestation of the power urge.

The power urge extends in its consequences beyond the desire for bodily selfhood. The paradox of the power urge is that its passion for singleness goes hand in hand with a desire for a leader. In *Love in the Western World*, De Rougemont describes the social and cultural situation in which Lawrence turned to the power idea.

> Love, in what till recently was called the post-war period, became a curious medley of anxious intellectualism—a number of novels then depicted dread and the middle-class defiance of restrictions—and of materialism—what the Germans called the *neue Sachlichkeit*. It was clearly recognized that romantic passion could no longer obtain the ingredients necessary to sustaining its myth, could no longer pick out flowers of resistance in the midst of an atmosphere charged with tempestuous and secret devotion. A pathological fear of

---

[40] Denis de Rougemont, *Love in the Western World*, trans. Montgomery Belgion (New York: Pantheon, 1956), p. 268. Jake Barnes, the hero of Hemingway's *The Sun Also Rises*, at once manly and sexually impotent, is an excellent instance of the ethos that De Rougemont is describing.

falling in love in a simple, straightforward manner and of suffering "deceptions of the heart" together with a feverish hankering after "experiences" formed the "climate" of the chief novels in vogue. The unambiguous significance of this was that *the individual relations of the sexes had ceased to be the most appropriate theater for passion to occur in.* Passion, it seemed was being detached from its concomitant. We entered upon a period of wandering *libidos* in quest of new spheres of activity. The first scene to offer itself was that of politics.[41]

To interpret Lawrence's view of the exhaustion of the love urge simply as an imaginative projection of his failure with Frieda is to deny that Lawrence shared a vision common to other writers of the age. To be sure, the fierce exchanges between Somers and Harriet in *Kangaroo* have a strong autobiographical charge, and Lawrence's failure (like Somers' with Harriet) to get Frieda to "submit" was, we know, a source of great pain to him. But whatever the circumstances of Lawrence's personal life might have been, Lawrence conceived them to be circumstances of the human condition at the contemporary moment.

"The wandering libido" in its involvement in politics represents Lawrence at his most vulnerable. The charge of fascism that has been leveled against him has its basis in part in these novels, in his affection for the power idea. Lawrence's attraction to the charismatic personality has embarrassing affinities with the mob's attraction to the fascist personality. The feline ferocity of a Don Ramon (*The Plumed Serpent*) made into a political principle can become an excuse for all sorts of atrocities, and to exalt the "primitive" in the political situation is to forget what might have happened to the "primitive" after so many centuries of psy-

---

[41] *Ibid.*, pp. 267–68.

chic repression. De Rougemont's *caveat* against "The Glorification of Instinct" is valuable—though it is not necessary to draw the same repressive conclusions that he draws.

> To plunge down below our moral rules is, therefore, not to abolish their restraints, but merely to indulge in more than animal insanity. The mistake lies in supposing that "the real thing," the longing for which has now become an obsession, is there to be found. It is not lying in wait for us on the far side of a surrender to enervated instinct and resentful flesh. It is not hidden, but lost. The only way to recover it is by building it up afresh, thanks to an effort that shall go against passion—etc.[42]

However, vulnerable as Lawrence is, the attempt to connect him with fascism is false to the facts of his thought and art. In *Kangaroo* the "fascist" leader is repudiated; in *The Plumed Serpent* the quality of Don Ramon's personal rule is finally different from fascism. The insistence on the personal and passional connection between man and man and man and woman is radically at odds with the immense machine that fascist political life becomes. Only a deliberate insensitivity to his intention can make for a reading that Lawrence is advocating a fascist program in the novel. To be sure, the desperate searches of Lawrence's heroes for leaders in *Aaron's Rod* and *The Plumed Serpent* make them susceptible to men of fascist persuasion. But Lawrence's heroes, desperate as they are, are without exception inviolable. They recoil immediately from political connections that will violate their singleness. It must not be forgotten that the novels that assert the power idea have as their principal theme the need for the hero to recover possession of his separate identity. The double quest for self-responsibility and for a leader is Lawrence's way of creating a balance that would obviate the vices of both quests.

---

[42] *Ibid.*, p. 237.

The leader checks the world-smashing impulse toward separateness, and the impulse toward separateness checks the tendency toward compulsion in the power relationship.

Power, as Lawrence conceives it, is the capacity to be single and self-sufficient (to recoil from "false inorganic connections"), but it has the corollary virtue of being able to impel the self to make *voluntary* connections with other vital beings. The political system of Don Ramon and Don Cipriano, despite its fatuous mystique and mumbo-jumbo, is based on a voluntary submission to the leader; in all the novels, one must remember, the follower characteristically seeks the leader and not the reverse. (When Aaron asks Lilly whom he should submit to, Lilly responds: "Your soul will tell you."[43]) Where the reverse is the case, the result is pernicious. Kangaroo's attempt to impose himself upon Somers meets with the necessary resistance, and the Laurentian Christ in *The Man Who Died* must learn, as he does, that death is the only consequence of trying to lay a compulsion upon men, even the compulsion of love.

Lawrence's conception of power is most deficient when he imagines it in its concrete political form. The new political system envisaged by Don Ramon and Don Cipriano, based on the sacrificial rites of an ancient cult of "the dark gods" mixed up with hymns that Lawrence sung as a boy in the Congregational Church that he attended, is, of course, an absurdity. Despite his criticism of Christ's self-sufficient asceticism in *Apocalypse*,[44] Lawrence, like Christ, rendered to Caesar earthly power by default.

Lawrence's continuous assault on money values, which he distinguished from life values, shows a characteristic in-

---

[43] *Aaron's Rod*, p. 290.

[44] See *Apocalypse* (New York: Viking Press, 1936), pp. 190–200.

sensitivity to the connection between power and money.[45] As Knight points out, it is one of the wisdoms of Shakespeare to recognize money and wealth as an opportunity for character to realize and express itself. "This gold-essence, the crown essence [Knight is characterizing the imagery of gold in Shakespeare], is to be equated with the sovereignty of the imagination itself, and must be directly referred also to the other, less reputable, gold of finance."[46] Lawrence's political imagination was either feeble or "hysterical." *The Plumed Serpent* has the appearance of an adolescent effort when placed alongside the great political novels: *The Red and the Black*, *The Charterhouse of Parma*, *The Possessed*, *The Secret Agent*. Lawrence's failure to think politically reflects his temperamental repugnance for automata in human life. The political intelligence, in its concern with the institutional arrangements by which men live, must consider human relationships in their depersonalized aspect—must consider men, in other words, as an abstraction or an "average" of the men that compose a class or a nation or a race. Lawrence was unable to think politically because he could not regard human relationships as anything other than *personal* relationships or *impersonal* encounters between the gods that inhabit two persons. The political novelist may share this repugnance for the depersonalizing character of politics, but the repugnance should not, if his vision of a political situation is to be illuminating, diminish his imaginative attention to it. When Lawrence conceives a political program, as he does in *The Plumed Serpent*, the searching critical intelligence of the novelist which discovers the incongruities between idea and action,

---

[45] Lawrence concludes *Apocalypse*, for instance, with a criticism of "our false, inorganic connections, especially those related to money" (p. 200).

[46] G. Wilson Knight, *Christ and Nietzsche* (London: Staples Press, 1948), p. 221.

intention and consequence, is suspended. He has, in other words, ceased to be a novelist and become a propagandist. After witnessing Don Ramon's career, it is difficult not to sympathize with his wife's outburst to Kate:

> "Power! Just power! Just foolish wicked power. As if there had not been enough horrible, wicked power let loose in this country. But he—he—he wants to be beyond them all. He—he—he wants to be worshipped. To be worshipped!"[47]

The violence, prominent in all his work, is particularly obnoxious in the political novels. The ugly streak of cruelty in both Don Ramon and Don Cipriano (in *The Plumed Serpent*) cannot be justified by an appeal to vital energy and nature. One must however distinguish between the artistic imagination of violence and the direct expression of it in life. Indeed, one can argue with Aristotle against Plato that art, rather than stimulating politically and socially subversive passions, purges or, in Freudian language, sublimates them. The distinction between art and life is, to be sure, a tangled question, and one could hardly expect to settle it here. When the imagination of violence is as extreme as it has been in the modern period—I need only cite the work and life of the contemporary novelist, Norman Mailer[48]—the distinction between art and life becomes a fine one indeed. Nevertheless, in Lawrence's case there is a distance between the thinking and the doing, and in any discussion of his "politics" that distance must be taken account of.

One is tempted to locate the source of the extravagances of Lawrence's political imagination in his failure to under-

---

[47] D. H. Lawrence, *The Plumed Serpent*, Introduction by Richard Aldington (London: William Heinemann, Ltd., 1955), pp. 161–62.

[48] See Norman Mailer, *Advertisements for Myself on the Way Out* (New York: Putnam, 1959), particularly the essay on "The White Negro."

stand paternal authority. In the essays on psychoanalysis the child is seen in its relationship to the mother, rarely to the father. Lawrence, of course, wrote out of bitter experience, and he understood that experience well enough to complain against the matriarchy that was developing in the modern world. But as he never had the opportunity to define himself in relation to paternal authority in his own life, he could never adequately imagine the right balance between freedom and authority in the political sphere.

Whatever Lawrence's deficiencies as a political novelist or thinker might be, it must be said that his fundamentally anti- or non-political temper kept him from the excesses into which a writer like Ezra Pound plunged. Lawrence, to be sure, wanted a *total* solution to the political mess of his time, and his impatience with that continuous exercise of political reason which is marked by tentativeness, clumsiness, and often mediocrity brought him to the verge of embracing "solutions" against which his whole being finally revolted. And he did revolt out of the wisdom that the totalitarian solution would be the death of all that he stood for. Lawrence's connection with personalities like John Hargrave (author of the "Kibbo Kift Kindred" movement) shows him to be susceptible but finally superior to the temptation. In a letter to Rolf Gardiner he praises some of Hargrave's ideas but attacks "his way—en masse."[49]

> If it weren't for his ambition and his lack of warmth, I'd go and kibbo kift with him. But he'll get no further than holiday camping and mummery. . . . All luck to him.—But by wanting to rope in *all* mankind it shows he wants to have his cake and eat it. Mankind is largely bad, just now especially, and

---

[49] *The Letters of D. H. Lawrence* (London: William Heinemann, Ltd., 1956), p. 700.

one must hate the bad, and try to keep what bit of warmth alive one can, among the few decent. . . .[50]

And in another letter to Gardiner, he even relinquishes the follower-leader ideal.

I'm afraid the whole business of leaders and followers is somehow wrong, now. . . . Leadership must die, and be re-born different, later on. I'm afraid part of what ails you is that you are struggling to enforce an obsolete form of leader-ship. It is White Fox's calamity. When leadership has died— it is very nearly dead, save for Mussolini and you and White Fox and Annie Besant and Ghandi—then it will be born again, perhaps new and changed and based on a reciprocity of ten-derness. The reciprocity of power is obsolete. When you get down to the basis of life, to the depth of warm creative stir, there is no power. It is never: There *shall* be light!— only; Let there be light! The same way, not: Thou *shalt* dance to the Mother Earth! only: Let it be danced to the mother earth.[51]

The repudiation of the follower-leader ideal and the new emphasis on a "reciprocity of tenderness" represent the final phase of Lawrence's career. Already in *The Plumed Serpent* Lawrence is recovering his old desire for connection and com-munity. The mood of "sheer repudiation," exploding the world, which Kate embodies (and which she shares with the heroes of the preceding novels, Aaron and Somers) gives way to the new urge in Kate to submit to the warmth and sexual authority of Don Cipriano. The love urge has, as it were, re-vitalized itself in Lawrence's imagination; it emerges to the surface in *The Man Who Died* and *Lady Chatterley's Lover* (the original title of which was *Tenderness*).

But the repudiation of the follower-leader relationship is not equivalent to a repudiation of the years during which Lawrence invoked the dark gods of *power*. The power urge

---

[50] *Ibid.*   [51] *Ibid.*, pp. 704–5.

was not a sudden invention; it crystallized something present in Lawrence's imagination from the very beginning of his career, and though he repudiated a particular manifestation of it when he rejected the follower-leader relationship, the power idea remains a permanent legacy of Lawrence's work.

Power in its deepest sense is the quiddity of the individual soul, which must be defended against every "ideal" attempt to distort its reality and diminish its potency. The quiddity of the soul is not always "the passionate life." Like Yeats, Lawrence knew that the worst are often full of "passionate intensity."[52] Indeed, he loathed the Dostoevskian characters[53] who he felt were "acting up, trying to *act* feelings because [they] haven't really got any."[54] And he much preferred the Hemingway characters of *In Our Time* to the Dostoevskian forcings of passion that he found in a good deal of contemporary Russian literature. Thus in a review of *In Our Time*, Lawrence speaks of "the healthy state of nothingness" in which Krebs lives.

> And he beats it, to somewhere else. In the end he'll be a sort of tramp, endlessly moving on for the sake of moving away from where he is. This is a negative goal, and Mr. Hemingway is really good, because he's perfectly straight about it. He is like Krebs, in that devastating Oklahoma sketch: he doesn't love anybody, and it nauseates him to pretend he does. He doesn't even *want* to love anybody; he doesn't want to go anywhere, he doesn't want to do anything. He wants just to lounge around and maintain a healthy state of nothingness inside himself, and an attitude of negation to everything outside of himself. And why shouldn't he, since

---

[52] See W. B. Yeats, "The Second Coming" (l. 8), *The Collected Poems of W. B. Yeats* (New York: Macmillan Co., 1958).

[53] How much of Lawrence's suspicion of Dostoevsky, one wonders, was born of self-mistrust?

[54] Review of *Fallen Leaves*, by V. V. Rozanov, *Phoenix: The Posthumous Papers of D. H. Lawrence* (New York: Viking Press, 1950), p. 389.

that is exactly and sincerely what he feels? If he really *doesn't* care, then why should he care? Anyhow, he doesn't.[55]

In Lawrence's novels and tales the hero will sometimes experience this healthy state of nothingness. It represents a moment in him when, perhaps tempted to falsify his situation, "to act up" to feelings that he does not have, he resists the easy temptation by preferring nothingness. Aaron's refusal to yield to the insistent demands of his wife for affection, because he simply can't find the affection within him, is one instance; another is the captain (of *The Captain's Doll*) incapable of love, accepting his incapacity cheerfully, even triumphantly. If we understand the power urge as the supreme court of appeal against every enticement, every coercion, every narcotic that might cheat a man of his true being, whatever it might be, then we have found its permanent place in Lawrence's metaphysic.[56] Lawrence's battle cry during "the middle period" of his career for resistance is finally a cry in behalf of "the maximum potentiality and splendour of the human species."[57] And the moralists who worry about Lawrence's egocentric morality might do well to heed the *caveat* of Nietzsche: ". . . Morality would really be saddled with the guilt, if the *maximum potentiality of the power and splendour* of the human species were never to be attained."

When Lawrence speaks of the obsolescence of "the reciprocity of power," he is again speaking in behalf of the soul's effort to protect itself against "ideal" distortions and diminu-

---

[55] Review of *In Our Time*, by Ernest Hemingway, *Phoenix*, p. 366.

[56] Thus Lawrence attached great value to the honest recording of vacuity, corruption, and sterility, which he was properly fastidious about having pure. Nothing evoked his critical ire more than intensity that was not experienced, emotions that were not felt. See review of *Fallen Leaves*, *Phoenix*, pp. 388–92.

[57] Friedrich Nietzsche, *The Genealogy of Morals*, trans. Horace B. Samuel, in *The Philosophy of Nietzsche*, p. 628.

tions of its reality. When power is *willed* or *forced* then it ceases to represent the soul in its true potency. Lilly of *Aaron's Rod* distinguishes his power doctrine from Nietzsche's will to power. Yet whatever misgivings Lawrence may have had about the Nietzschean insistence on the *will* to power, he would have doubtless agreed with Nietzsche's characterization of the cardinal instinct of organic being. "A living thing seeks above all to *discharge* its strength."[58] Power in this sense is present, as we shall see, in the new "reciprocity of tenderness" that is born out of the ashes of the follower-leader ideal.

II

The Man Who Died[59] is the masterpiece of Lawrence's "final period," the period in which Lawrence conceived the new "reciprocity of tenderness." It is a kind of grand summation of Lawrence's principal themes, a revelation of the strengths and weaknesses of his utopian ambitions.

The Man Who Died begins on an ironic note. Lawrence's Christ is miraculously recalled to life by a "loud and splitting" cock crow.[60] Pained and disillusioned, the man discovers that the world that he had denied for the illusory glory of eternal life has its own undying glory. "The world, the same as ever, the natural world, thronging with greenness, a nightingale singing winsomely, wistfully, coaxingly calling from the bushes beside a runnel of water, in the world, the natural world of morning and evening, forever undying, from which he had died."[61]

With his keen religious intuition, Lawrence has subtly per-

---

[58] Nietzsche, *Beyond Good and Evil*, in *The Philosophy of Nietzsche*, p. 395.

[59] *The Man Who Died* was not Lawrence's title; in editions published during his lifetime the book had its true title "The Escaped Cock."

[60] *Ibid.*, p. 4.   [61] *Ibid.*, p. 6.

ceived the *religious* heresy of the Christian impulse toward self-transcendence. By trying to exceed the reach of his hands and feet in order to achieve communion with God—in order perhaps to become God—man is separated from God and diminished in the separation. The nausea, the emptiness and disillusion that the man who died suffers are the "rewards" Lawrence imagines for the sacrilege. Lawrence is presenting in a new way the old paradox of the Christian critique of the Renaissance conception of man—namely, that the centering of the universe around man makes for a diminution of his stature. As Lawrence exploits the paradox, however, man in his full splendor and potency is conceived by Lawrence according to the Renaissance model. For Lawrence, as for every true religious writer, the imagination of divinity and the imagination of the self are inextricably bound together. As the imagination of divinity fails, so does the imagination of the self. Lawrence's loathing of modern literature derives from a feeling that it offers us the spectacle of small selves in a godless universe, attempting to achieve significance through the magnification of their most trivial feelings. (". . . it is self-consciousness, picked into such fine bits that the bits are most of them invisible, and you have to go by the smell. Through thousands and thousands of pages Mr. Joyce and Mrs. Richardson tear themselves to pieces, strip their emotions to the finest threads."[62])

The effect of Lawrence's contempt for "the idiotic foot-rule" that "man is the measure of the universe"[63] is a kind

---

[62] *Phoenix*, p. 518.

[63] In a letter to Trigant Burrow, Lawrence writes the following: "People are too dead and too conceited. *Man is the measure of the universe.* Let him be it: idiotic foot-rule which even then is *nothing.* In my opinion, one can never *know:* and never-never *understand.* One can but swim like a trout in a quick stream . . ." (*The Letters of D. H. Lawrence*, p. 635). This is a very compressed statement of Lawrence's view of the humanist presumption. The fatality of consciousness is that it separates man from the world, compels him to regard him-

of misanthropy. In *The Man Who Died*, for instance, the repudiation of Christ's mission to convert men to the God of Love ("to lay the compulsion of love on all men") is accompanied by an intense hatred of the City of Man.

> So he went his way, and was alone. But the way of the world was past belief, as he saw the strange entanglement of passions and circumstance and compulsion everywhere, but always the dread insomnia of compulsion. It was fear, the ultimate fear of death, that made men mad. So always he must move on, for if he stayed, his neighbors wound the strangling of their fear and bullying around him. There was nothing he could touch, for all, in a mad assertion of ego, wanted to put a compulsion on him, and violate his intrinsic solitude. It was the mania of cities and societies and hosts, to lay a compulsion upon a man, upon all men. For men and women alike are mad with the egoistic fear of their own nothingness.[64]

We are reminded in the above passage of Lawrence's kinship with other misanthropes: Swift and Nietzsche, for example. The misanthropy is obviously connected with Lawrence's attraction to the "inhuman" and the "impersonal": the cosmic energy before individuation in its condition of mystery. Throughout his work there is a fascination with the undomesticated "inhuman" quality of his characters.

The action of *The Man Who Died* is the painful recovery of the God in the body, which culminates in the man's passionate embrace of the priestess of Isis. The fierce and raging physical life that had earlier seemed resistant now responds to their passion.

> All changed, the blossom of the universe changed its petals and swung round to look another way. The spring was ful-

---

self, and makes the moment of self-regard, as it were, the meaning of the world. Also, see Wallace Fowlie, *Jacob's Night: The Religious Renaissance* (New York: Sheed & Ward, 1947), p. 72.

[64] *The Man Who Died*, in *The Short Novels*, II, 22.

filled, a contact was established, the man and the woman were fulfilled of one another.[65]

Significantly, the priestess of Isis is abandoned at the end of *The Man Who Died*, having fulfilled her role as the conduit to the mysteries of "the greater life of the body."

If Lawrence is averse to Christianity, there remains nonetheless his deep attraction to the figure of Christ. Lawrence's Christ retains the chastity, the purity of soul that marks the Christ of the gospels. Before his embrace of the priestess of Isis there had been a long and difficult "rebirth," in which the man had learned "the irrevocable *noli me tangere* which separates the reborn from the vulgar." Christ's misguided chastity is turned into a strength. Like the other Laurentian heroes, Aaron and Somers, the man who died must resist the lure of false, self-diminishing connections. Before his meeting with the priestess of Isis, he undergoes a kind of purification in which he relives his old experiences—with humanity, "particularly with humanity in authority,"[66] with Madeleine, with Judas. (The purification recalls Blake's aphorism in *The Marriage of Heaven and Hell*: "If the doors of perception were cleansed everything would appear to man as it is, infinite."[67])

The tenderness between the man and the priestess is not the sentimentalism of a new love code. The touch of the priestess heals the man's wounds, but more than that it connects the man with the living universe and restores to him a sense of power. Indeed, the fulfilment between the man and the priestess is short-lived, for "departure was in the air."[68] And the man's departing words to the priestess recall the in-

[65] *Ibid.*, p. 44.

[66] *Ibid.*, p. 7.

[67] William Blake, *The Marriage of Heaven and Hell*, in *The Portable Blake* (New York: Viking Press, 1953), p. 264.

[68] *The Man Who Died*, in *The Short Novels*, II, 44.

sistence in *Fantasia of the Unconscious* on the necessity of the daylight world, where a man can be with other men or alone on the frontier of the unknown.

> "I must go now soon. Trouble is coming to me from the slaves. But I am a man, and the world is open. But what is between us is good, and is established. Be at peace. And when the nightingale calls again from your valley-bed, I shall come again, sure as spring."[69]

Though the man "would go alone, with his destiny,"[70] the priestess' touch will be upon him and will be, as it were, the bond that guarantees his return to her in the spring.

The aloneness theme persists even at the moment of Lawrence's new imagination of "the reciprocity of tenderness," and it is the mark of the importance of the preceding phase of Lawrence's career when his people were in sharp recoil from connections with others. The inhuman and nihilistic tendency in Lawrence's work required the check that came from his sensuousness. But the tendency is present in *The Man Who Died*, though in a more humanized form, and the essential egocentrism of Lawrence's imagination is as strong as ever.

> "I have sowed the seed of my life and my resurrection, and put my touch forever upon the choice woman of this day, and I carry her perfume in my flesh like essence of roses. She is dear to me in the middle of my being. But the gold and flowing serpent is coiling up again, to sleep at the root of my tree."[71]

The egocentrism is humanized not only by the sensuousness, but also by a new note of humility. The humility is evident only if one reads *The Man Who Died* as a double allegory on Lawrence himself as well as on Christ. The man's speech to Madeleine, for instance, unmistakably registers a personal note.

---

[69] *Ibid.*, pp. 45–46.   [70] *Ibid.*, p. 45.   [71] *Ibid.*, p. 47.

"But my mission is over, and my teaching is finished and
death has saved me from my own salvation. Oh Madeleine, I
want to take my single way in life, which is my portion. My
public life is over, the life of my self-importance."[72]

One cannot avoid having in mind the frail, red-bearded writer
with the messianic sense. Lawrence is here rejecting not only
Christ's particular mission, but also the self-created legend
that had its absurd apotheosis in the notorious "last supper"
at the Café Royale. But if Lawrence assumed the messianic
role, he soon learned its bitter fruits. There were plenty of
Judases within his own circle, and like the man of the Christ
story, Lawrence learned how much he himself was responsible for the betrayals he experienced. There are anticipa-
tions of Lawrence's abdication of the messianic role in his
letters, admissions that his doctrine of spontaneity and individual being was compromised by the categorical impera-
tives that he was constantly issuing. In a letter to Lady Cyn-
thia Asquith, Lawrence recognizes his own impulse to lay
compulsions upon other people—to dictate *his* spontaneous
feelings to others.

And never again will I say, generally, "the war"; only "the
war to me." For to every man the war is himself, and I cannot dictate what the war is or should be to any other being
than myself. Therefore I am sorry for all my generalities,
which must be falsities to another man, almost insults. Even
Rupert Brooke's sonnets which I repudiate for myself, I
know how true it is for him, for them.[73]

No art, especially one with a strong prophetic intention,
can avoid the "generalities" which Lawrence vows to es-
chew. In *Lady Chatterley's Lover*, for instance, though he has
presumably given up trying to change the world, the simple
presentation of a relationship between lovers reflects Lawrence's urging of a change of consciousness that he would

---

[72] *Ibid.*, p. 13.   [73] *The Letters of D. H. Lawrence*, p. 379.

want to become universal. Indeed, art—even when it is most private or when its subject is the most intimate relationships between people—is, because of its public character, an action in the world. An art, however, that springs from acute mistrust of the public world, that has learned the lesson of how the self is compromised in its action in the world and that chooses in its alienation to cultivate an understanding of the intimate and personal lives of men, is caught on the horns of a dilemma. How is it to protect itself from the consequences of its publicity? Lawrence's savage portrait of Hermione, a "Laurentian personality," comes out of just such an awareness. And so do the countless letters written during Lawrence's dark period in which he counseled hiding and retreating.

> Shelter yourself above all from the world, save yourself, screen and hide yourself, go subtly in retreat, where no one knows you . . . hiding like a bird, and living busily the other creative life, like a bird building a nest. . . .[74]

And yet if the dilemma can never really be resolved, it is nevertheless true that the human activity that suffers least from the dilemma is art, because it is the only human activity that can preserve the "illusion" of privacy even in its public aspect. "The single way of life" that the man who died chooses is a choice that we are all urged to make, and as such "the mission" has simply taken another form, but "the compulsion" to choose the single way depends upon the individual reader, who will be moved only if he feels that the man has made the choice out of his own experience and suffering and not as part of the writer's design to persuade him. In other words, the degree to which a work is the incarnation of one's creative life, which for Lawrence takes place in "hiding," the more powerful will be its effect on the lives of the people it touches.

---

[74] *Ibid.*, p. 375.

The ambiguous relationship between Christ and the law gave Lawrence, as it gave Blake and Dostoevsky, a unique opportunity to present his claims for "the single way of life." If Christ comes to fulfil the law, he comes also to destroy the version of the law—whatever it may be—that prevails in the world. Blake's Christ assimilates to himself the energies of Hell in order to destroy the life-killing "rules" that govern the human spirit: "I tell you, no virtue can exist without breaking these ten commandments. Jesus was all virtue, and acted from impulse, not from rules."[75] And Dostoevsky's Christ brings the gift of complete spiritual freedom, because the Church which bears His name has taken it away from mankind in exchange for mystery, miracle, and authority.[76] The opposition between Christ and the law in its worldly embodiment is the opposition between vital spirit and dead matter, between freedom and coercion, spontaneity and compulsion. If it is the nature of the world to turn energy into matter, power into weakness, the spirit into the word, then Christ exists as the permanent possibility of the renewal of energy, power, and spirit. Though he has no permanent abode in the world, there is always the possibility of his return.

Indeed, from this point of view even Nietzsche, the great "antichrist" of modern culture, is, as G. Wilson Knight has pointed out, "analogous to Christ himself in [Christ's] challenge against the rigidity of Judaic Law."[77] Knight has very brilliantly argued for the Dionysian, or power, content of Christ's doctrine as opposed to the Christian doctrine. Thus he distinguishes between the inclusive "super-sexuality" of Christ and "the ghostly, bloodless, nasalised and utterly un-

---

[75] Blake, *The Marriage of Heaven and Hell*, in *The Portable Blake*, p. 258.

[76] See Lawrence, Introduction to "The Grand Inquisitor," *Phoenix*, pp. 283–91.

[77] Knight, *Christ and Nietzsche*, p. 119.

sexual . . . tone of our Church tradition."[78] Jesus' dread of
the crowd, his impulse to solitude, and the pain and joy of the
crucifixion and resurrection are regarded by Knight as the
Dionysian involvement with the cosmos that carries the self
beyond the "normal" sexual and sensual experience of the
world into a hermaphroditic oneness of the self with the universe, of the self with the self. Thus Christ's love is not al-
truism, but self-renewal. Viewed from this "higher critical"
position, Lawrence's *The Man Who Died* is a great retelling
of the story within the tradition.

But Lawrence's version, in which the man separates himself from the vulgar after he descends from the cross, is a repudiation of something central in the *Christian* ethos. Lawrence has seen through the *willed* democratic character of
Christianity and rejected it for a fierce aristocratic aloneness.
Whatever ultimate significance the life of Jesus had—and it
is reasonable to regard Jesus himself as in a sense anti-Chris-
tian—Christianity for writers like Blake, Nietzsche, and
Lawrence had come to be an enemy of life, and the attempts
of commentators and critics to reconcile them to Christianity
on some higher ground have the effect of depriving them of
the weapon that Jesus himself was permitted: the sword. Like
Christ, Lawrence came with the sword. His message was not
peace and reconciliation, but destruction and re-creation. The
gentle Jesus who embodied the hopes and aspirations of the
meek and the poor (the Jesus of Christianity) is an alien
spirit to Lawrence.

In an introduction that Lawrence wrote to Dostoevsky's
version of the Christ story, the un-Christian and aristocratic
power bias of Lawrence's imagination is confirmed in an extraordinary way. In summarizing the argument of the Grand
Inquisitor, Lawrence makes his characteristic effort to rescue

---

[78] *Ibid.*, p. 210.

the tale from the artist. According to Lawrence, Christ's kiss, which is paralleled in the Karamazov story by the kiss Ivan receives from Alyosha, is a kiss of acquiescence in the rightness of the Grand Inquisitor's argument. "Ivan had made a rediscovery of a truth that had been lost since the eighteenth century."[79] The truth, which puts the lie to the rationalist belief in the perfectibility of all men, is that the burden of freedom can be endured by the gifted, unhappy few who must assume the burden for the rest of mankind. Lawrence very shrewdly observes that the Grand Inquisitor's argument is close to the Christian idea of a single man supremely endowed, assuming the burden for all mankind. But we are kept from seeing the resemblance by the dramatic situation, the "cynical Satanical"[80] pose that the Grand Inquisitor is made to affect. He is presumably in league with the Devil, and the fact that "the wise [humane] old man"[81] has been made to put on the garb of the terrible Inquisitor of the auto-da-fé distracts us from the wisdom and the humanity of his argument.

Lawrence turns the Grand Inquisitor's argument into a justification of his mistrust of what Nietzsche calls "the herd" and of the necessity of protecting the freedom and power of the few from the presumption that all men are capable of perfection.

> So let the specially gifted few make the decision between good and evil and establish the life values against the money values. And let the many accept the decision, with gratitude, and bow down to the few, in the hierarchy.[82]

Lawrence wrote the article when the political possibility was still open to him. In *The Man Who Died* the public life is renounced, but the aristocratic and Nietzschean bias remains.

---

[79] Introduction to "The Grand Inquisitor," *Phoenix*, p. 290.
[80] *Ibid.*, p. 283.   [81] *Ibid.*, p. 290.   [82] *Ibid.*

It is, of course, a curious fact that Lawrence sides with the Grand Inquisitor against Christ, though for reasons different from those that explain Lawrence's affinity with Christ elsewhere. There is throughout Lawrence a fear that the doctrine of spontaneity and freedom will be perverted by those for whom freedom is an excuse for self-indulgence and coercion. Lawrence's willingness to send Dostoevsky's Christ away is a salutary warning to his readers of the danger that his own work embodies. His misanthropy, paradoxically, keeps him from wanting his doctrine to become the property of all men. Lawrence's "political period" immediately preceding *The Man Who Died* was very instructive in this respect. The hero of *Kangaroo*, for instance, learns that he must repudiate political connections that will violate his singleness. There is a qualifying humility in Lawrence (a consequence of his religious character perhaps) which keeps him from sharing Blake's and Nietzsche's belief in the power of men (even the best of them) to transcend themselves infinitely. Lawrence mistrusted what Mark Schorer has called (writing of Blake) the politics of vision. His respect for human limitations counteracted the anarchic Dionysian tendency of his imagination. His work at moments seems a balance of opposing tendencies, and this balance gives the impression of health and normality, which critics like F. R. Leavis make so much of. Even in Lawrence's fierce repudiations and self-affirmations, the imagination of distinction, relation, balance, and hierarchic order often appears. Nevertheless, Lawrence is *essentially* like Blake and Nietzsche in his address to the untapped powers of man and his hatred of the rules and forms that curb those powers.

A Representative Destiny

Jaspers' characterization of the achievement of Kierkegaard and Nietzsche is suggestive in evaluating Lawrence's impact on the modern world.

> With them, a new form of reality appears in history. They are, so to speak, representative destinies, sacrifices whose way out of the world leads to experiences for others. They are by the total staking of their whole natures like modern martyrs, which, however, they precisely denied being. Through their character as exceptions, they solved their problem.
>
> Both are irreplaceable, as having dared to be shipwrecked. We orient ourselves by them. Through them we have intimations of something we could never have perceived without such sacrifices, of something that seems essential which even today we cannot adequately grasp. It is as if the Truth itself spoke, bringing an unrest into the depths of our consciousness of being.[1]

The characters of whom Jaspers speaks must enact their destiny no matter what the risks may be, and that destiny is to remain faithful to a vision which may defy what Lawrence called "the little fold of law and order." It is, of course, necessary to qualify Jaspers' claim for Kierkegaard and Nietz-

---

[1] Karl Jaspers, in Walter Kaufmann (ed.), *Existentialism: From Dostoevsky to Sartre* (New York: Meridian Books, 1959), p. 174.

sche in relation to Lawrence. Unlike the two European thinkers, Lawrence is not a "world historical" figure. To be sure,
he has a place of importance in world literature, but it is only
in England and America that he is truly a "representative
destiny."

In America and England, even the hostility to him is generally an act of self-definition. One has only to contrast the
brief discussion of Lawrence in Simone de Beauvoir's *The
Second Sex*[2] with the essays of Diana Trilling[3] or the work of
William York Tindall.[4] In Mme de Beauvoir's book Lawrence, despite his extraordinary sympathy with the female
consciousness, is simply another (and rather unimportant) example of the way in which the male novelist considers the
woman as secondary ("other") in a relationship. Mrs. Trilling, on the other hand, records the enthusiasm of a whole
generation for Lawrence and her more recent misgivings
about him are seen in terms of the cultural history of the past
three decades. Whatever her doubts about Lawrence, her
essays register with remarkable clarity Lawrence's importance in the Anglo-American consciousness. And the animus
of Mr. Tindall's book is precisely his irritation at the enthusiasm that Mrs. Trilling describes.[5]

During the dark hours of Lawrence's reputation in Eng-

---

[2] Simone de Beauvoir, *The Second Sex*, trans. and ed. H. M. Parshley (New York: Alfred A. Knopf, 1953), pp. 214–22.

[3] See Diana Trilling (ed.), Introduction to *The Portable Lawrence* (New York: Viking Press, 1950), pp. 1–32; and Introduction to *Selected Letters of D. H. Lawrence* (New York: Farrar, Straus & Cudahy, 1958), pp. xi–xxxvii.

[4] See William York Tindall, *Lawrence and Susan His Cow* (New York: Columbia University Press, 1939); and the essay on *The Plumed Serpent*, in *The Achievement of D. H. Lawrence*, eds. Frederick J. Hoffman and Harry T. Moore (Norman: University of Oklahoma Press, 1953), pp. 178–84.

[5] In his introductory essays to *The Plumed Serpent* and *The Later D. H. Lawrence*, Professor Tindall has shown himself to be more sympathetic with Lawrence's intentions and achievement than he was in *D. H. Lawrence and Susan His Cow*.

land, the hostility or indifference toward him was a significant cultural fact. As a bête noire to writers like T. S. Eliot and Wyndham Lewis, he was an "irreplaceable" figure on the English scene.[6] Leavis' championship of Lawrence during those dark hours was again the fulfilment of Lawrence's "representative destiny." Lawrence's visits to Cambridge, where he met Russell, Keynes, and other members of the Bloomsbury set and found them all "dead, dead, dead,"[7] are re-enacted, so to speak, by Leavis and the group that he leads in their indictment of Bloomsbury culture. The conclusion of Leavis' book on Lawrence underlines the extent to which Leavis has accepted Lawrence as a figure to which he has oriented himself, and therefore to which we must orient ourselves if we are to perceive the essential truths of our world.

> [Lawrence] has an unfailingly sure sense of the difference between that which makes for life and that which makes against it; of the difference between health and that which tends away from health. . . . But I ought at this point to add that I speak as one who, when years ago Mr. Eliot wrote in *The Criterion* of the frightful consequences that might have ensued if Lawrence "had been a don at Cambridge, 'rotten and rotting others,' " was widely supposed—at Cambridge, anyway, where it mattered—to share the honor of the intention with Lawrence.[8]

Lawrence's parochialism derives in part from the Puritan character of his mind. His rootlessness and eternal wandering might have counteracted this parochialism, had it not been for the opacity of his genius, which transformed every

---

[6] See Eliot, *After Strange Gods: A Primer of Modern Heresy* (New York: Faber & Faber, Ltd., 1934); and Wyndham Lewis, *Paleface: The Philosophy of the "Melting Pot"* (London: Chatto, 1929).

[7] See *D. H. Lawrence: A Composite Biography*, ed. Edward Nehls (Madison: University of Wisconsin Press, 1956–59), I, 282.

[8] F. R. Leavis, *D. H. Lawrence: Novelist* (New York: Alfred A. Knopf, 1956), p. 393.

place he visited into a manifestation of his primal vision of the universe. Even Frieda Lawrence's sympathetic introduction to *Lady Chatterley's Lover* registers the view that the novel is "the last word in Puritanism."[9] And Norman O. Brown, who has dedicated himself to the reconstruction of the Dionysian ego, speaks disparagingly of Lawrence as "that paradoxically conservative philosopher of sexuality"[10] and makes scant subsequent mention of him.

Brown is responding in his own fashion to the strong Puritan strain in Lawrence, who insisted on the right moral and religious conditions for acts of passion.

> Never "use" venery at all. Follow your passional impulse, if it be answered in the other being; but never have any motive in mind, neither off-spring nor health nor even pleasure, nor even service. Only know that "venery" is one of the great gods. An offering-up of yourself to the very great gods, the dark ones, and nothing else.[11]

The discriminations that Lawrence makes among various kinds of sexual experience, the relentlessness with which he pursues the battle against pornography, the extent to which his characters often are in flight from women—all this goes to substantiate the claim about Lawrence's Puritanism. And one might add that Lawrence is as prohibitive as he is prescriptive; for every "Thou shalt!" there is a "Thou shalt not!"

Lawrence's didacticism, his moral urgency, his impatience with art itself have precedents in writers as different from one another as Milton, Blake, and George Eliot. Even his positive attitude toward the passions has its sanction in the Protestant

---

[9] Frieda Lawrence, Introduction to *The First Lady Chatterley* (New York: Dial Press, 1944), p. v.

[10] Brown, *Life against Death* (Middletown, Conn.: Wesleyan University Press, 1959), p. 181.

[11] *Studies in Classic American Literature* (New York: Doubleday Anchor Books, 1953), p. 28.

tradition. Luther himself, we may remember, restored the marriage sacrament to the religious and moral life out of his belief in the inextricable connection between passion and life itself.

> The sexual is, undoubtedly, Luther's main impulsive force and problem at once. "What is needed to live in continence," he says, "is not in me"; and again, "Just as I have not power not to be a man, so it does not lie in my power to live without a woman." He writes against chastity and considers desire unconquerable even by marriage, so winning over to his theology "the impatient sensuality of his day."[12]

One of the impulses of Protestantism is to integrate the passional and the moral lives by conceiving the passional life in a state of innocence. For that a myth is needed, and this myth is readily supplied by the Bible. Milton's use of the story of the Garden of Eden is, of course, the greatest expression in England of the Protestant imagination. Blake's *Songs of Innocence* and *Songs of Experience* and George Eliot's use of the pastoral tradition in *Adam Bede*, in which she conceived an identity between natural and social law, are other instances. Lawrence too is drawn to the myth:

> Man ate of the tree of knowledge, and became ashamed of himself.
>
> Do you imagine Adam had never lived with Eve before that apple episode? Yes he had. As a wild animal with his mate.
>
> It didn't become "sin" till the knowledge-poison entered. The apple of Sodom.
>
> In the first place, Adam knew Eve as a wild animal knows its mate, momentaneously, but vitally, in blood knowledge.
> . . . Blood-knowledge, instinct, intuition, all the vast vital flux of knowing that goes on in the dark, antecedent to the mind.

---

[12] G. Wilson Knight, *Christ and Nietzsche: An Essay in Poetic Wisdom* (London: Staples Press, 1948), p. 3.

> When Adam went and took Eve, *after* the apple, he didn't do any more than he had done many a time before. . . . Before the apple, they had shut their eyes and their minds had gone dark. Now, they peeped and pried and imagined. They watched themselves. And they felt uncomfortable after. They felt self-conscious. So they said, "The *act* is sin. Let's hide. We've sinned."[13]

Before Eve ate the apple poison there had been no sin: the myth of unfallen man is Lawrence's antidote to the apple poison. And its moral intention is not the antinomianism that appears on first glance. The myth is part of Lawrence's strenuous effort to overcome evil. He is not so much proposing a wild abandonment to passion as he is trying to connect passion to the moral and religious life. This is the meaning of his imagination of primal innocence, for the time before "the fall of man" was a time when man walked in the presence of gods, and angels were his daily visitors. Lawrence shows himself to be a child of civilization when he identifies sex with tenderness or even with deity, for such identifications are made in the wisdom that sex is a powerful energy that is never in the pure state in the human realm. The identification of sex with tenderness or with the gods is a channeling of sexual energy, not a way of impoverishing sex—a guarantee that sex will not become a species of narcissism or sadism. Of course, this is only part of the truth about Lawrence.

Lawrence's "representative destiny" has not yet been fully appreciated. At the heart of that destiny is "the knot of contrariety" of which his thought and art are made. His need for positive assertion, his rhetorical and incantatory impulse, sometimes prevented him from making the necessary confrontation of the oppositions in his thought and art. Cosmic oneness and separateness, consciousness and mindlessness,

---

[a] *Studies in Classic American Literature*, p. 94.

passion and intelligence, love and power, perversity and health: these oppositions suggest the dialectical character of Lawrence's imagination.

No account of Lawrence's belief in the living cosmos which includes nature, mankind, nation, and family can ignore the profound, willed rootlessness of his life, the feeling often displayed by his characters, as well as by himself in his letters, that to stay in any one place would only dry up the source of his creativity. Nor can the demonstration of the "normative" character of his vision leave out of account the Dionysian perversities into which his characters are sometimes plunged and to which we are made witness in an imaginative atmosphere of strange moral neutrality, even at times approval; nor can we fail to keep in mind his extremist tendencies, which at times make Lawrence's belief in order, balance, and measure seem like the desperate ideals of a man trying to emerge from his agony. His open hostility to intellectual consciousness is qualified by the fact that in conceiving new ideas through the unremitting resistance to habitual patterns of thought and feeling Lawrence was performing the radical task of intellect. And the egocentric power ethic that he evolved must be understood vis-à-vis his strong erotic sensuousness. Similarly, the dark gods toward which Lawrence's imagination was urged are to be remembered when we consider the biblical atmosphere of *The Rainbow*, the nonconformist tradition out of which Lawrence came.

These are not the oppositions of a mind uncertain about its interests and convictions; rather they are the oppositions of a man who tried to incarnate in his life and work the opposing tendencies of his culture. The impulse toward integration was too strong and too impatient in Lawrence for him to achieve the success he wanted. Wilson Knight, envisaging the possible integration of the Puritan and passional strains of the English personality, cites Nazi Germany as an instance of the "poison" that "lies secreted" in integration, "the mechanisms of integration being its own last and most deadly obstacles."[14] Knight writes of Germany:

> Its eternity-craving is partial and irresponsible, without due respect for the nature of past and future, that is, for time; especially for the slowness of time. It is over-hasty, like Lady Macbeth's ambition, trying to "seize the future in the instant." . . . (Germany appears powerful in instinct and transcendental perception), but weak in those integrating factors, which should serve to compact these, which are (i) the sense of sin, a recognition of inward discrepancy in time, fear of one's past or future not acceptable to the present judgment; and (ii) the sense of humour, a recognition of discrepancy in simultaneity and therefore, we may say, in space.[15]

Earlier in the book, Knight, interestingly enough, singled out Lawrence as the English writer who embodies implicitly the Dionysian power urge that culminated in naziism. (". . . we can see the work of D. H. Lawrence as one burningly self-conscious moment in this great movement of the European imagination."[16]) One hesitates to accept the full implications of Knight's view of Lawrence, simply because it disregards the resistances in Lawrence himself to the political consequence of the power urge. Lawrence's Puritan conscience, his doctrine of self-responsibility, the stubborn English strain in his temperament, protected him from committing himself to the madness that overtook Germany. But Knight's identification of Lawrence with naziism points to the real problem that confronts modern culture and which Lawrence and

---

[14] Knight, *Christ and Nietzsche*, p. 232.

[15] *Ibid.*, p. 230.   [16] *Ibid.*, p. 57.

others have faced in various ways. How does one reconcile the urgency of energy and passion with the demands of civilized life—order, obligation, etc.? In Nietzsche's language, how does one achieve the necessary harmony between the Apollonian and the Dionysian impulses?

In addressing ourselves to this question, we may be able to cut through the knot of contrariety to a view of the *essential* Lawrence without sacrificing his complexity. Lawrence is neither a "normative" writer, judging life from some conventional standard of health or vitality, nor is he a perverse writer, reveling in a fantasy that defies or deviates from the norms of civilization. Like Blake and Nietzsche before him, Lawrence has managed to see and judge the quality of life (its norms and its perversities) from a vantage point outside of civilization. Such a statement is of course meaningless to those who deny the existence of such a vantage point. We may remember De Rougemont's statement: "To plunge down below our moral rules is . . . not to abolish their restraints, but merely to indulge in more than animal insanity. The mistake lies in supposing that 'the real thing,' the longing for which has now become an obsession, is there to be found."[17] As a *caveat* against the dangers of "the glorification of instinct," this statement is valuable, but as a theoretical statement about human possibility, it seems to me presumptuous and unacceptable. To regard the moral rules as absolutes against which there is no radical appeal is both to indulge in the humanistic presumption that this is the best of all possible worlds and to invalidate a priori any radical criticism of the norms of a civilization. It is to reject as valueless the visionary genius.

Lawrence's mistake was to confuse the visionary and the

---

[17] Denis de Rougemont, *Love in the Western World* (New York: Pantheon, 1956), p. 237.

ethically prescriptive. His vision of life finally should not be taken as a guide to conduct, the hortatory, preacherish manner of much of his work notwithstanding. The urging to follow "one's deepest impulse" is either nonsensical or dangerous, for given the human condition impulsiveness would sooner issue in horror than in vitality. Only those in a state of grace can be trusted to follow their deepest impulses. And these aristocrats of the spirit (artists, heroes, saints) need no exhortation, for they must follow these impulses by virtue of what they are. When Lawrence converts his vision into doctrine and turns prophecy into moral prescription, he betrays a confusion about his achievement. The visionary habit is alien to the moral life, because it refuses to accommodate itself to anything different from it. To confuse the visionary and the ethical is to hold out a false promise to the *demos* (everyone can have a vision if he would only care), a temptation that even the visionary artist finds hard to resist in a democratic society. To be a "Laurentian" is not a simple matter of cherishing "the warm life" and valuing spontaneity. (The cult of the Laurentian is a reductive appropriation of Lawrence.)

The power of the visionary artist for us is in his autonomy, in his exclusive love of the mysterious and the inchoate, in what Lawrence called his otherness. He does not have the spirit of community. He may regret it and long for it as Lawrence did, but it is a futile longing, for the spirit of community is foreign to his character. And because of this the visionary artist has within him an extraordinary power of judgment. If we listen to him, we may be kept from the *hubris* of complacency and self-congratulation, of a facile faith in humanity and civilization. To write him off as a dangerous fellow then is to do a disservice not only to "life," but to the human community as well—indeed, it is to make intolerable the very

idea of human life. But he *is* a dangerous fellow, and it is difficult not to sympathize with De Rougemont especially since
the spirit of the age has come to be in many ways a horrible
parody of that same Dionysian element that is supposed to
inspire the artist.

Of course, Lawrence did not see the opposition between
the visionary and the ethical as a necessary one. His opposition to Freud, for instance, reflects his refusal to tolerate this dualism. For Freud, in his characteristic view, a natural harmony between impulse and civilization is impossible
of achievement. Civilization, an Apollonian product, depends
on the repression or the sublimation of the passional energies.

> ... civilization has been built up, under the pressure of the
> struggle for existence, by sacrifices in gratification of the
> primitive impulses, and it is to a great extent forever be-
> ing re-created, as each individual successively joining the
> community, repeats the sacrifice of his instinctive pleasures
> for the common good. The sexual are amongst the most im-
> portant of the instinctive forces thus utilized; they are in this
> way sublimated, that is to say, their energy is turned aside
> from its sexual goal and diverted towards other ends, no
> longer sexual and socially more valuable.[18]

The tension between impulse and repression (between the
visionary and the moral) that exists within both the individual
and culture is a permanent tension to which man must accommodate himself. The tragic or pessimistic tone of Freud's
later work reflects his view that the passional self and the re-

---

[18] Sigmund Freud, *General Introduction to Psychoanalysis*, trans. Joan Riviere
with a preface by Ernest Jones and G. Stanley Hall (New York: Perma Giants,
1949), pp. 23–24. As Norman O. Brown has pointed out, there is an am-
biguity in the Freudian concept of sublimation. Whereas in the passage
cited above, sublimation is conceived almost as a synonym of repression,
Freud elsewhere characterizes sublimation as "a way out, a way by which
the claims of the ego can be met without involving repression." Brown, *Life
against Death*, p. 139. Freud's characteristic view, however, is represented by
the passage above.

quirements of civilized life are in permanent opposition to each other. In *Civilization and Its Discontents,* in which Freud complicates this view by the postulation of the aggressive instincts and the death wish, the opposition is not simply between impulse and repression, but also between Eros (the sublimation of the sexual instinct) and Thanatos (the destructive and disintegrative force in civilization). The possibility of harmony is embodied by Eros, "builder of cities," but Eros is only one term of the opposition in Freud's Manichean vision of civilization.

> The fateful question of the human species seems to me to be whether and to what extent the cultural process developed in it will succeed in mastering the derangements of communal life caused by the human instinct of aggression and self-destruction. In this connection, perhaps the phase through which we are at this moment passing deserves special interest. Men have brought their powers of subduing the forces of nature to such a pitch that by using them they could now very easily exterminate one another to the last man. They know this—hence arises a great part of their current unrest, their dejection, their mood of apprehension. And now it may be expected that the other of the two "heavenly forces," eternal Eros, will put forth his strength so as to maintain himself alongside his equally immortal adversary.[19]

In *Fantasia of the Unconscious* Lawrence rejects Freud's dualism and claims for the religious-creative faculty—that faculty which builds civilization—the character of impulse. The impulse is even deeper than—and not necessarily at odds with—the sexual impulse. The opposition between Apollo and Dionysus is then a perverse contrivance of civilization in its present form, and the violence and destructiveness of the passional life is a function of the opposition between the gods,

---

[19] Freud, *Civilization and Its Discontents,* trans. Joan Riviere (New York: Jonathan Cape & Harrison Smith, 1930), pp. 143–44.

not a generic truth about the passional life itself. Lawrence conceives of culture in its ideal form as a fulfilment of the passional-visionary self. The destructiveness of the passions is really their resentment at the repression from which they have suffered. Moreover, Lawrence often attributes destructive violence—as distinguished from the creative violence, which brings new life forms into being—to the "mechanical" will which tries to impose the repressive "ideals" of the present civilization on the passional life.[20]

Lawrence never tells us how we can recover an unresentful passion after all those years of repression. Though he may be able to resolve the dualism in argument, Lawrence's imaginative work reveals the opposition between the visionary and the ethical at every moment. "Never trust the artist, trust the tale." Lawrence's argument reads like the casuistry against which he directed his fire when he discovered it in other writers. But it is a casuistry with which we must sympathize, for it reflects the anxious atmosphere in which he worked: the need to connect with others, to participate in the community of mankind, was in keen struggle with the need to keep faithful to a vision that was anarchically individual, explosive, and subversive. His impulse to argue for the vision represents an effort to join, in Malraux's phrase, his "madness to the universe." We respect the vision, but we cannot embrace it as doctrine. Between Lawrence and every serious reader of him there must be, I believe, a permanent tension: a sense of provocation and danger.

Lawrence is, like Blake and Nietzsche, an artist beyond good and evil who compels our admiration and mistrust. Like

---

[20] The violent deaths of Banford in *The Fox* and the captain in "The Prussian Officer" are instances of creative violence, the cruelty of the captain toward the orderly in "The Prussian Officer" and of 'Rico toward St. Mawr of destructive violence.

Christ, Lawrence enters the human community a stranger and an enemy, possessed by a vision so subversive and dangerous that he can be endured only if he modifies it in communicating it—or if he is misunderstood. Lawrence does modify his vision and he has been, understandably, misunderstood: that is, made to serve the gods of a humanistic civilization. This too, has been the fate of Blake and Nietszche.

Bibliography

I Works of D. H. Lawrence in the Phoenix Edition with Introductions by RICHARD ALDINGTON

Aaron's Rod. London: William Heinnemann, Ltd., 1954.
The Complete Poems. 3 vols.; London: William Heinemann, Ltd., 1957.
The Complete Short Stories. 3 vols.; London: William Heinemann, Ltd., 1957.
Kangaroo. London: William Heinemann, Ltd., 1955.
Lady Chatterley's Lover. London: William Heinemann, Ltd., n.d.
The Lost Girl. London: William Heinemann, Ltd., [1920].
Mornings in Mexico and *Etruscan Places*. London: William Heinemann, Ltd., 1956.
The Plumed Serpent. London: William Heinemann, Ltd., 1955.
The Rainbow. London: William Heinemann, Ltd., 1957.
Sea in Sardinia. London: William Heinemann, Ltd., 1956.
The Short Novels. 2 vols.; London: William Heinemann, Ltd., 1956.
Sons and Lovers. London: William Heinemann, Ltd., [1913].
The Trespasser. London: William Heinemann, Ltd., [1912].
Twilight in Italy. London: William Heinemann, Ltd., 1956.
The White Peacock. London: William Heinemann, Ltd., [1911].
Women in Love. London: William Heinemann, Ltd., 1957.

II Other Books by D. H. Lawrence

A Collier's Friday Night. Introduction by EDWARD GARNETT. London: M. Secker, 1934.
Apocalypse. Introduction by RICHARD ALDINGTON. New York: Viking Press, 1936.
Assorted Articles. London: M. Secker, 1930.

D. H. Lawrence: Selected Literary Criticism. Edited by ANTHONY BEAL. New York: Viking Press, 1955.

The First Lady Chatterley. Introduction by FRIEDA LAWRENCE. New York: Dial Press, 1944.

Lady Chatterley's Lover (the third manuscript version, first published by Giuseppi Orioli, 1928). Introduction by MARK SCHORER. New York: Grove Press, 1959.

The Later D. H. Lawrence. Selected with an Introduction by WILLIAM YORK TINDALL. New York: Alfred A. Knopf, 1959.

The Letters of D. H. Lawrence. Edited with an Introduction by ALDOUS HUXLEY. London: William Heinemann, Ltd., 1956.

Phoenix: The Posthumous Papers of D. H. Lawrence. Edited with an Introduction by E. D. McDONALD. New York: Viking Press, 1950.

The Portable Lawrence. Edited with an Introduction by DIANA TRILLING. New York: Viking Press, 1950.

Psychoanalysis and the Unconscious and *Fantasia of the Unconscious.* Introduction by PHILIP RIEFF. Compass Books; New York: Viking Press, 1960.

Selected Letters of D. H. Lawrence. Edited with an Introduction by DIANA TRILLING. New York: Farrar, Straus & Cudahy, 1958.

Sex, Literature and Censorship. Edited with an Introduction by HARRY T. MOORE. Compass Books; New York: Viking Press, 1953.

Studies in Classic American Literature. New York: Doubleday Anchor Books, 1953.

Touch and Go: A Play in Three Acts. New York: T. Seltzer, 1920.

The Widowing of Mrs. Holroyd. New York: M. Kennerley, 1914.

III   Books on Lawrence

ALDINGTON, RICHARD. *D. H. Lawrence: Portrait of a Genius But.* New York: Duell, Sloan & Pearce, 1950.

FREEMAN, MARY. *D. H. Lawrence: A Basic Study of His Ideas.* New York: Grosset & Dunlap, 1955.

GREGORY, HORACE. *The Pilgrim of the Apocalypse: A Critical Study of D. H. Lawrence.* New York: Viking Press, 1934.

HOFFMAN, FREDERICK J., and MOORE, T. HARRY (eds.). *The Achievement of D. H. Lawrence.* Norman: University of Oklahoma Press, 1953.

Hough, Graham. *The Dark Sun: A Study of D. H. Lawrence.* New York: Capricorn Books, 1956.

Lawrence, Frieda. *"Not I, but the Wind . . ."* London: William Heinemann, Ltd., 1935.

Leavis, F. R. *D. H. Lawrence: Novelist.* New York: Alfred A. Knopf, 1956.

Moore, Harry. *The Intelligent Heart: The Story of D. H. Lawrence.* New York: Farrar, Straus & Young, 1954.

——— (ed.). *A D. H. Lawrence Miscellany.* Carbondale: Southern Illinois University Press, 1959.

Murry, Middleton. *Son of Woman: The Story of D. H. Lawrence.* New York: Jonathan Cape & Harrison Smith, 1931.

Nehls, Edward (ed.). *D. H. Lawrence: A Composite Biography.* 3 vols.; Madison: University of Wisconsin Press, 1956–59.

Spilka, Mark. *The Love Ethic of D. H. Lawrence.* Bloomington: Indiana University Press, 1957.

Tindall, William York. *Lawrence and Susan His Cow.* New York: Columbia University Press, 1939.

Tiverton, Father William. *D. H. Lawrence and Human Existence.* London: Rockliff Publishing Corporation, Ltd., 1951.

Vivas, Eliseo. *D. H. Lawrence: The Failure and the Triumph of Art.* Evanston: Northwestern University Press, 1960.

West, Anthony. *D. H. Lawrence.* London: Arthur Barker, Ltd., 1950.

IV General Works

Abrams, M. H. (ed.). *Essays on English Romantic Poets.* New York: Oxford University Press, 1960.

Allen, William. *The English Novel.* New York: E. P. Dutton & Co., 1958.

Auden, W. H. *The Collected Poetry of W. H. Auden.* New York: Random House, 1945.

Auerbach, Eric. *Mimesis.* Translated by Willard Trask. New York: Doubleday Anchor Books, 1957.

Austen, Jane. *The Complete Novels of Jane Austen.* New York: Modern Library, n.d.

Bantock, Granville. *Freedom and Authority in Education.* London: Faber & Faber, 1952.

BARZUN, JACQUES. *Romanticism and the Modern Ego.* Boston: Little, Brown & Co., 1943.

BEACH, JOSEPH WARREN. *The Concept of Nature in Nineteenth Century English Poetry.* New York: Pageant Book Co., 1956.

BEAUVOIR, SIMONE DE. *The Second Sex.* Edited and translated by H. M. PARSHLEY. New York: Alfred A. Knopf, 1953.

BENTLEY, ERIC RUSSELL. *A Century of Hero-Worship.* Philadelphia: J. B. Lippincott Co., 1944.

BERDYAEV, NICHOLAS. *Dostoevsky.* Translated by DONALD ATTWATER. New York: Meridian Books, 1959.

BERGSON, HENRI. *The Two Sources of Morality and Religion.* Translated by R. A. AUDRA and CLOUDESLEY BRERETON. New York: Doubleday Anchor Books, 1957.

BLACKMUR, R. P. *Form and Value in Modern Poetry.* New York: Doubleday Anchor Books, 1957.

BLAKE, WILLIAM. *The Portable Blake.* Edited with an Introduction by ALFRED KAZIN. New York: Viking Press, 1953.

BOWRA, C. M. *The Heritage of Symbolism.* London: Macmillan & Co., Ltd., 1947.

BRADLEY, A. C. *Shakespearean Tragedy.* London: Macmillan & Co., Ltd., 1950.

BROWN, NORMAN O. *Life against Death.* Middletown, Conn.: Wesleyan University Press, 1959.

CAMUS, ALBERT. *The Stranger.* Translated by STUART GILBERT. New York: Vintage Books, 1956.

CASSIRER, ERNST. *Essay on Man: An Introduction to a Philosophy of Human Culture.* New Haven: Yale University Press, 1944.

———. *Language and Myth.* New York and London: Harper & Bros., 1946.

CAUDWELL, CHRISTOPHER. *Studies in a Dying Culture.* London: John Lane, 1948.

CONRAD, JOSEPH. *The Secret Sharer* and *Heart of Darkness.* Introduction by ALBERT J. GUERARD. New York: New American Library, 1958.

COOK, ALBERT. *The Meaning of Fiction.* Detroit: Wayne University Press, 1960.

DOSTOEVSKY, FYODOR. *The Best Short Stories of Dostoevsky.* Translated with an Introduction by DAVID MAGARSHACK. New York: Modern Library, n.d.

————. *The Brothers Kamarazov.* Translated by CONSTANCE GAR-
NETT. New York: Modern Library, 1950.

ELIOT, GEORGE. *Adam Bede.* Introduction by GORDON HAIGHT.
New York: Rinehart & Co., 1958.

————. *Middlemarch.* Edited with an Introduction by GORDON
HAIGHT. Boston: Riverside Press; Cambridge: Houghton Mifflin
Co., 1956.

ELIOT, T. S. *After Strange Gods: A Primer of Modern Heresy.* New
York: Faber & Faber, Ltd., 1934.

ELLMAN, RICHARD. *Yeats: The Man and the Masks.* New York:
Macmillan Co., 1948.

FAULKNER, WILLIAM. *Light in August.* Introduction by RICHARD
H. ROVERE. New York: Modern Library, 1950.

————. *The Sound and the Fury.* New York: New American Library, 1959.

FIEDLER, LESLIE A. *No! in Thunder: Essays on Myth and Literature.* Boston: Beacon Press, 1960.

FLAUBERT, GUSTAVE. *Madame Bovary.* Edited with an Introduction
by CHARLES I. WEIR, JR. Translated by ELEANOR MARX AVELING.
New York: Rinehart & Co., 1957.

FOWLIE, WALLACE. *Jacob's Night: The Religious Renaissance in
France.* New York: Sheed & Ward, 1947.

FREUD, SIGMUND. *The Basic Writings of Sigmund Freud.* Edited and
translated with an Introduction by A. A. BRILL. New York:
Modern Library, 1938.

————. *Beyond the Pleasure Principle.* Translated by C. J. M. HU-
BACK. London: Hogarth Press and the Institute of Psychoanalysis, 1948.

————. *Civilization and Its Discontents.* Translated by JOAN RIVIERE.
New York: Jonathan Cape & Harrison Smith, 1930.

————. *Future of an Illusion.* Translated by W. D. ROBSON-SCOTT.
London: Horace Liveright and the Institute of Psychoanalysis,
1928.

————. *A General Introduction to Psychoanalysis.* Translated by
JOAN RIVIERE with a Preface by ERNEST JONES and G. STANLEY
HALL. New York: Perma Books, 1949.

————. *Group Psychology and the Analysis of the Ego.* Translated by
JAMES STRACHEY. London: Hogarth Press, 1948.

HARDY, FLORENCE EMILY. *The Later Years of Thomas Hardy 1892–1928.* New York: Macmillan Co., 1930.

HARDY, THOMAS. *Jude the Obscure.* New York: Modern Library, 1923.

———. *The Return of the Native.* New York: Modern Library, 1927.

———. *Tess of the d'Urbervilles.* Introduction by CARL J. WEBER. New York: Modern Library, 1951.

———. *The Woodlanders.* London: Macmillan & Co., 1949.

HARTMAN, GEOFFREY. *The Unmediated Vision: An Interpretation of Wordsworth, Hopkins, Rilke and Valéry.* New Haven: Yale University Press, 1954.

HEMINGWAY, ERNEST. *The Old Man and the Sea.* New York: Charles Scribner's Sons, 1952.

———. *The Sun Also Rises.* New York: Charles Scribner's Sons, 1954.

HUGHES, H. STUART. *Consciousness and Society: The Reorientation of European Social Thought 1890–1930.* New York: Alfred A. Knopf, 1958.

HUXLEY, ALDOUS. *Brave New World.* New York and London: Harper & Bros., 1946.

JASPERS, KARL. *Man in the Modern Age.* Translated by EDEN and CEDAR PAUL. New York: Doubleday Anchor Books, 1957.

JOYCE, JAMES. *The Portable Joyce.* Edited with an Introduction by HARRY LEVIN. New York: Viking Press, 1946.

———. *Ulysses.* New York: Modern Library, 1946.

KAUFMANN, WALTER (ed.). *Existentialism: From Dostoevsky to Sartre.* New York: Meridian Books, 1959.

———. *Nietzsche: Philosopher, Psychologist, Anti-Christ.* New York: Meridian Books, 1959.

KNIGHT, G. WILSON. *Christ and Nietzsche: An Essay in Poetic Wisdom.* London: Staples Press, 1948.

LEAVIS, F. R. *The Great Tradition.* New York: Doubleday Anchor Books, 1954.

LEWIS, WYNDHAM. *Paleface: The Philosophy of the 'Melting Pot.'* London: Chatto, 1929.

MAGNUS, MAURICE. *Memoirs of the Foreign Legion.* Introduction by D. H. LAWRENCE. London: M. Secker, 1924.

MAILER, NORMAN. *Advertisements for Myself on the Way Out.* New York: Putnam, 1959.

MANN, THOMAS. *Stories of Three Decades*. Translated by H. T. Lowe Porter. New York: Alfred A. Knopf, 1948.

MARCUSE, HERBERT. *Eros and Civilization: A Philosophical Inquiry into Freud*. Boston: Beacon Press, 1955.

MONTGOMERY, JOHN. *The Twenties, an Informal Social History*. New York: Macmillan Co., 1957.

NIETZSCHE, FRIEDRICH. *The Philosophy of Nietzsche*. Introduction by WILLARD HUNTINGDON. New York: Modern Library, 1950.

―――. *The Use and Abuse of History*. Translated by ADRIAN COLLINS. New York: Library of Liberal Arts, 1957.

―――. *The Will to Power*. Translated by ANTONY M. LUDOVICI. 2 vols.; New York: Macmillan Co., 1924.

ORWELL, GEORGE. *1984*. New York: Harcourt, Brace & Co., 1949.

PATER, WALTER. *Appreciations*. London: Macmillan & Co., Ltd., 1924.

PEGUY, CHARLES. *The Temporal and the Eternal*. Translated by ALEXANDER DRU. 2 vols.; New York: Harper & Bros., 1958.

PICK, ROBERT (ed.). *German Stories and Tales*. New York: Pocket Library, 1959.

RILKE, RAINER MARIA. *Duino Elegies*. The German text with an English translation. Introduction and commentary by J. B. LEISHMAN and STEPHEN SPENDER. New York: W. W. Norton & Co., Inc., 1939.

―――. *The Journal of My Other Self*. Translated by M. D. HERTER NORTON and JOHN LINTON. New York: W. W. Norton & Co., Inc., 1930.

―――. *Letters to a Young Poet*. Translated by M. D. HERTER NORTON. New York: W. W. Norton & Co., Inc., 1934.

―――. *Sonnets to Orpheus*. Translated by M. D. HERTER NORTON. New York: W. W. Norton & Co., Inc., 1942.

―――. *Wartime Letters*. Translated by M. D. HERTER NORTON. New York: W. W. Norton & Co., Inc., 1940.

ROE, F. W. (ed.). *Victorian Prose*. New York: Ronald Press, 1947.

ROUGEMONT, DENIS DE. *Love in the Western World*. Translated by MONTGOMERY BELGION. New York: Pantheon, 1956.

SARTRE, JEAN PAUL. *Existentialism and the Human Emotions*. Translated by BERNARD FRECHTMAN and HAZEL E. BARNES. New York: Philosophical Library, 1957.

SCHORER, MARK. *William Blake: The Politics of Vision.* New York: Henry Holt & Co., 1946.

SHELLEY, PERCY BYSSHE. *Essays and Letters.* Edited with an Introductory Note by ERNST RHYS. Garden City, N.Y.: Garden City Publishing Co., 1943.

SPENDER, STEPHEN. *The Destructive Element: A Study of Modern Writers and Beliefs.* London: Jonathan Cape, 1935.

STENDHAL. *The Red and the Black.* Translated by LOWELL BAIR with an Introduction by CLIFTON FADIMAN. New York: Bantam Books, 1958.

SWIFT, JONATHAN. *Gulliver's Travels and Other Works.* London: Oxford University Press, 1956.

TINDALL, WILLIAM YORK. *The Literary Symbol.* Bloomington: Indiana University Press, 1955.

TOLSTOY, LEO. *The Short Novels of Tolstoy.* Edited with an Introduction by PHILIP RAHV. Translated by AYLMER MAUDE. New York: Dial Press, 1956.

TRILLING, LIONEL. *Freud and the Crisis of Our Culture.* Boston: Beacon Press, 1955.

VAN GHENT, DOROTHY. *The English Novel: Form and Function.* New York: Rinehart, 1953.

VERGA, GIOVANNI. *Cavalleria Rusticana and Other Stories.* Translated by D. H. LAWRENCE. London: Jonathan Cape, 1928.

VIVANTE, LEONE. *A Philosophy of Potentiality.* London: Routledge, 1955.

WATT, IAN. *The Rise of the Novel.* Berkeley and Los Angeles: University of California Press, 1957.

WHITE, F. R. (ed.). *Famous Utopias of the Renaissance.* New York: Hendricks House, 1955.

WHITEHEAD, ALFRED NORTH. *Adventures of Ideas.* New York: Macmillan Co., 1937.

———. *Alfred North Whitehead: An Anthology.* Edited by F. S. C. NORTHROP and MASON W. GROSS. New York: Macmillan Co., 1953.

WILLIAMS, RAYMOND. *Culture and Society.* New York: Columbia University Press, 1958.

WILSON, EDMUND. *Axel's Castle.* New York: Scribner & Sons, 1931.

WORDSWORTH, WILLIAM. *The Complete Poetical Works of William Wordsworth*. London: Macmillan & Co., 1903.

YEATS, W. B. *The Collected Poems of W. B. Yeats*. New York: Macmillan Co., 1958.

———. *A Vision*. New York: Macmillan Co., 1956.

V   Articles

GOODHEART, EUGENE. "Freud and Lawrence," *Psychoanalysis and the Psychoanalytic Review*, XLVII (Winter, 1960), pp. 56–65.

McCARTHY, MARY. "The Fact in Fiction," *Partisan Review*, XVII (Summer, 1960), 438–58.

TRILLING, LIONEL. "The Modern Element in Modern Literature," *Partisan Review*, XXVIII (January–February, 1961), 9–35.

TROY, WILLIAM. "The Lawrence Myth," *Partisan Review*, IV (January, 1938), 3–13.

WIDMER, KINGSLEY. "D. H. Lawrence and the Art of Nihilism," *Kenyon Review*, XX (Autumn, 1958), 604–16.

Index